TECHNOLOGICAL
INNOVATION IN CHINA

TECHNOLOGICAL INNOVATION IN CHINA
The Case of the Shanghai Semiconductor Industry

DENIS FRED SIMON
DETLEF REHN

BALLINGER PUBLISHING COMPANY
Cambridge, Massachusetts
A Subsidiary of Harper & Row, Publishers, Inc.

This book has been supported by the Stiftung Volkswagen Foundation in Hanover, West Germany.

International Standard Book Number: 0-88730-206-8

Library of Congress Catalog Card Number: 88-24121

Printed in the United States of America

Library of Congress Cataloging-in-Publication Data

Simon, Denis Fred.
  Technological innovation in China : the case of the Shanghai semiconductor industry / Denis Fred Simon, Detlef Rehn.
    p.   cm.
  Bibliography: p.
  Includes index.
  ISBN 0-88730-206-8
  1. Semiconductor industry—China—Shanghai. 2. Technological innovations—Economic aspects—China—Case studies. 3. Industry and state—China—Case studies. I. Rehn, Detlef. II. Title.
HD9696.S43C675   1988
338.4'7621381'09—dc19   88-24121

CONTENTS

LIST OF FIGURES

LIST OF TABLES

ACKNOWLEDGMENTS

Undertaking a research project as complex and difficult as this is not an easy task. Numerous persons in China were kind enough to assist us in arranging interviews, collecting data, and discussing a host of issues pertaining to the book. This book is dedicated to those people in China who see the actual and potential value to their country of increased interaction with the outside world. We are particularly indebted to the Shanghai Academy of Social Sciences and Fudan University for acting as our sponsors in Shanghai. We would also like to express our gratitude to the former mayor of Shanghai, Wang Daohan, who had the vision to see that a study such as this could be mutually beneficial to China and the foreign business and scholarly communities.

Primary funding for this project came from the Volkswagen Foundation in West Germany. Without their generosity this study would not have been possible. Other assistance was provided by the Office of Technology Assessment of the U.S. Congress and the Committee for Scholarly Communication with the People's Republic of China of the U.S. National Academy of Sciences.

To Melissa and Mitchell who have only just begun to understand why their daddy and his friends keep running off to China.

INTRODUCTION

The death of Mao Zedong in 1976 marked an important turning point in the economic and technological history of China. Since Mao's departure, major changes have taken place in China's approach to and strategy for economic development and technological modernization. Science and technology, which were the object of political attack during the Cultural Revolution, are now held in high esteem. Mental labor has been rehabilitated, and is now on an equal, if not higher, plane than manual labor. Scientific and technical personnel are being moved into positions of authority. And China appears embarked on its own version of a technological revolution.

One truly significant aspect of the current move to modernize the economy and to stimulate technological innovation is the emphasis being placed on high technology. It is not so much that China has abandoned so-called traditional industries or that it has advanced so rapidly that high-technology industries are its next logical frontier to challenge. Rather, the emphasis on high technology in China today represents its attempt to gain entry into the international division of labor at a level more commensurate with the industrialized nations than with other developing countries. China not only seeks to close the prevailing technological gap between itself and the United States, Western Europe and Japan—it also wishes to "catch up." In this regard, Deng Xiaoping's China may bear many resemblances to Japan—both in the Meiji era and in the post–World War II period. Obviously, the circumstances are different, as are some of the national imperatives. Nonetheless, high-technology for China ensures that the Chinese economy and its people will not be left behind as new and more rapid technological changes take place in other parts of the world.

There are also a host of internal factors that seem to be driving this entire process. The notion of establishing regional centers of excellence and high economic and technological performance as a form of specialization also constitutes a break from the previous policy of local self-sufficiency. By moving away from extreme forms of vertical integration towards more horizontal cooperation and interaction, the Chinese hope to restructure their economic processes. They also hope to restructure the institutions that were responsible for the problems of inefficiency, low productivity, and uneven growth that plagued the economy in the past. Cities such as Shanghai, with their strong industrial and R&D foundations, which historically have played a prominent role in supporting the national economy, are being counted on to propel the economy in new and different ways than heretofore was the case. The idea, for example, of creating a number of Silicon Valley-like sites in China reflects this new emphasis on regional strengths and capabilities.

This book originated, in large part, because of these new policies and the desire to understand better their potential impact on China's modernization. More specifically, we initially assumed that if China's high technology objective was to be launched anywhere on the Chinese mainland, it would first be in a setting such as Shanghai. This is not to deny the multiplicity of problems the city has faced over the last several years. Since 1984 Shanghai's position in industry has been declining. Jiangsu province assumed the number one position in industrial output in mid-1985. Nonetheless, Shanghai, perhaps propelled by a growing recognition of its weaknesses, has remained firmly committed to transforming its basic manufacturing and technology base and utilizing its substantial production and R&D resources to restore its leadership position in the economy. When combined with the fact that Beijing has placed enormous pressure on Shanghai to modernize its plant and equipment as well as spearhead the country's export drive, a case study of Shanghai seemed ideal for gaining a micro-level understanding of China's policy-making process.

Moreover, electronics was chosen as the focus of the book because of the strategic importance attached to this industry by Chinese leaders, a rather ironic twist in view of the somewhat neglected, highly politicized treatment electronics received during the heyday of most of Mao's stay in power. By viewing Chinese industrial policy and innovation-related behavior through the lens of electronics, we believed that we could gain important insights into the workings of the Chinese system, the extent to which reforms were indeed proceeding ahead, and the degree to which the Chinese were experiencing bottlenecks—organizational, techno-logical, political, and economic—in their move to revitalize the elec-tronics industry.

Innovation was deemed to be of primary importance for a number of reasons. First, China was focusing on innovation and technological change at a somewhat similar time as the United States and several Western European nations were re-examining their own approaches to this issue in the context of rising Japanese competition and slower domestic growth within the respective nations. Second, China's own stated objectives include not merely just a willingness to utilize foreign technology but—more significantly—a desire to increase national self-reliance. Foreign technology import is not seen as an end in itself but rather as a means to stimulate local innovation and technological ad-vance. Under such circumstances, one could argue that foreign technology may be a necessary element in China's modernization pro-gram, but without a local innovative capability, it is far from being a sufficient factor.

Third, China has instituted a number of major reforms in its science and technology system (see below) that promise to alter the requisites and process of innovation. The March 1985 Central Committee Deci-sion on Reform of the Science and Technology Management System marks a revolution in terms of the broad range of changes that have been introduced into Chinese R&D activities, especially in terms of the way technology is viewed and the way research activities are financed. Taken together, all three of these considerations made innovation a natural object of study in the context of the electronics industry.

Materials for this book have come from a number of sources. The major part of the materials have come via interviews conducted by the authors during a six-week stay in Shanghai in July 1985 and a three week stay in Beijing in January 1986. A list of the facilities visited is provided in the Appendix. In addition, interviews have been conducted with numerous visiting Chinese delegations to the U.S. and the Federal Republic of Germany. Statistical data have been extremely difficult to secure, particularly if one is concerned about the reliability of Chinese-supplied data. Statistical information about the electronics sector is often hard to collect because of the military-related linkages of the sector.

Nonetheless, the authors have found the *China Statistical Yearbook,* the *China Economic Yearbook,* and the *Mechanical and Electronics Industries Yearbook,* and the recently published *China Electronics Industry Yearbook* to be extremely valuable. We have also come to depend on a number of key Chinese newspapers and magazines, including *Zhongguo Dianzi Bao, Jisuanji Shijie, Shijie Jingji Daobao, Dianzi Shichang, Guoji Dianzi Bao,* and *Jingji Ribao.* Finally, we have also benefited from reading newspapers such as the *China Daily, Asian Wall Street Journal,* and *South China Morning Post* and magazines such as *JETRO China Newsletter, China Trade Report, China Business Review, Business China,* and *Beijing Review.*

1 INNOVATION IN CHINA
A Historical Perspective

INNOVATION IN PLANNED ECONOMIES

From the initial inception of the People's Republic in 1949, the task of promoting scientific advance and technological innovation has been of paramount importance. Immediately after liberation, the leadership began to devote its attention to the creation of a workable science and technology (S&T) infrastructure. This included both the restoration of the former Academia Sinica, hereafter referred to as the Chinese Academy of Sciences (CAS), and the establishment of a set of new R&D institutions in the industrial sector. The major objective of these efforts was to make certain that research and production were strongly integrated. The scientific community was constantly admonished to ensure that its research had some practical and immediate applications. Ironically, these same themes continue to occupy the attention of Chinese leaders as they prepare for China's entry into the high-technology world of the twenty-first century.

Historically, the problems of innovation have taken on a special character in planned economies. Unlike in the West, the innovation process is not embedded in a web of market-type relationships. The fundamental barriers to innovation are generically different; they are not simply a function of the economies of scale in research or production, cost advantages associated with factory input and capital, or product

1

differentiation. Similarly, the stimuli underlying innovation are also typically different. Nancy Dorfman suggests, for example, that in the market-driven system,

> if it [a firm] is to have an incentive to invest in the R&D for a new product it must expect to receive a price greater than the unit cost of production to include a return on R&D as well, and that return will have to be as great as the firm could expect to earn on any other resources, including compensation for the often very considerable risk that is involved in launching a new product.[1]

In planned systems, innovation tends to be part of a larger administrative hierarchy whose R&D efforts are more the product of highly directed resource mobilization than a response to market signals. The driving forces behind innovation generally have less to do with capturing projected surpluses or accepting greater risks in anticipation of high returns than with attaining a variety of more collective goals. In many cases, this has had a major influence on the pattern and character of industrial development in planned economies such as in the Union of Soviet Socialist Republics (USSR) and in Eastern Europe.[2] In these countries, leaders have faced the dilemma of having to stimulate rapid and sustained technological progress while at the same time preserving an appreciable degree of administrative control over economic affairs and research endeavors. The sustained tension between the imperatives of control and innovation helps to explain the generally low level of overall technological performance in planned economies as well as the direction of reform efforts since the 1960s. The experience of the USSR, in particular, has shown this.[3]

Technological innovation can be viewed as that process by which human and capital resources combine to create knowledge and technical ideas that can be translated into new or enhanced products, manufacturing processes and services.[4] The results of innovation may include radical or incremental change. Moreover, technological innovation also involves various forms of organizational change and adaptation, which may be either the cause or the result of the innovation process. Studies of the innovation process tend to point out that it is neither smooth nor linear, though success in technical problem solving depends upon the steady acquisition of relevant experience over the course of time.[5]

In the existing literature, there continues to be widespread disagreement about the requisites for successful innovation.[6] Nonetheless, a number of things can still be noted about the determinants of the process. The capacity for innovation depends not simply upon an organization's technological prowess, but also upon the nature of the organization itself and the external environment in which it operates.[7] Organizations vary not merely in terms of size and function, but also in terms of the locus of idea generation, the resources available for innovative activity, the nature of authority structures, the patterns of communication, and the grouping of personnel and physical resources. Each organization develops its own internal "culture"; in some cases, this culture may retard as well as facilitate innovative activities and behavior.[8]

Similarly, the climate for technological innovation is also a function of a number of external factors, including the political environment, the industrial structure, the financial system, and the nature of social and economic incentives.[9] Taken together, these factors embody a set of dominant values that will either provide a continual raison d'être for engaging in innovation-related activities or lead economic actors to forgo such considerations.[10] In market-driven economies, the desire for profit tends to be the main motivation behind technological innovation. Most innovation is of a "demand-pull" nature, that is, it is driven by market demands. Schumpeter's entrepreneur, spurred on by the dynamics of competition, embodies the demand-pull type of innovative behavior.[11]

In situations where the market is either absent or immature, technology push may be the more common force behind innovation. This is not to deny the role that technology push sometimes plays in a market-driven setting. Rather, where market pressures are weak, other innovation-generating forces may be at work, such as national prestige or military sponsorship. On some occasions, both types of stimuli, push and pull, may be missing insofar as definitions of acceptable economic performance or organizational effectiveness are narrowly stated, e.g. meeting an output quota, and do not necessarily include the ability to introduce new technologies or refine existing ones. Under such circumstances, innovation-related behavior may not occur on a regular or consistent basis, if it occurs at all. Nor will there be the supporting infrastructure necessary to move new ideas (hardware and software) from formulation to implementation and application.

Just as significant as the problems of generating innovation in planned economies has been the problem of the diffusion and transfer of innovation.[12] Domestic technology transfer can be classified in two basic ways.[13] First, technology may be transferred either vertically or horizontally. Vertical transfer occurs when know-how is conveyed from basic and applied research *to* development and production. Horizontal transfer takes place when the technology and information employed in one location is transmitted or diffused for application in another location. In centrally run economic systems, the engine behind such transfers is also usually an administrative decision. Part of the reason for reliance on this mechanism is because technology and know-how are treated, for the most part, not as commodities, but rather as public goods belonging to society and not private individuals or organizations. Only recently have such institutions as patents and copyrights begun to develop in most planned economies. The primary impetus has been an external one, that is, the desire to engage in international trade or attract foreign investment and technology.

The second method of distinguishing technology transfer, which has both a domestic and international dimension, has to do with the nature of the "package" being provided. Specifically, three types of transfer packages can be differentiated: (1) material transfer, which consists of the transfer of materials, components, and final products or equipment; (2) design transfer, which consists of the movement of the designs, blueprints, and ability to manufacture designated products or equipment, i.e. technology adoption; and (3) capacity transfer, which involves the adaptation of acquired technology and know-how to local conditions. As the experience of the newly industrialized nations indicates, formal as well as informal mechanisms for each of the three types of transfer must exist if the benefits of innovation are to be broadly realized within a country, especially ones as large as the Soviet Union and China. These mechanisms include everything from a viable system for information dissemination and publication to channels for the relatively free movement of scientific and technical labor.[14] Even if these mechanisms operate according to administrative fiat, they must be sufficiently underwritten by appropriate incentives and economic management techniques to make the transfers happen.[15]

THE CHINESE CASE

Commenting on the problems of innovation within the USSR, Berliner suggests,

> the structure of economic organization, like that of resource allocation in general, is not to be explained as the result of a general market-like socioeconomic

process. That structure is the result of an administrative decision, taken to be sure, with certain economizing in mind, but not influenced in turn by the actions of competing organizational units. The decision, taken early in Soviet history, was to locate the knowledge-production process primarily in units that are independent of the enterprises that introduce the new knowledge into production.[16]

This has resulted in the evolution of a research system with only ordered links to the industrial sector.

A similar set of conclusions regarding the R&D system in planned economies is reached by Amann and Cooper in an assessment of innovative performance in the USSR. Among the various factors affecting the climate for innovation in the Soviet Union, they cite two prominent constraints: (1) the economic system is permeated by departmental barriers, which impede cooperation between industrial ministries and tend to isolate scientific activity from manufacturing activity; and (2) there is a systematic tendency on the part of industrial enterprises and their ministries to maximize output at the expense of quality and novelty of products and thus to attach a relatively low priority to industrial innovation.[17] As a result, industrial managers, who would otherwise be the main end-users of new products and production processes, have tended to eschew the adoption of new technologies as these new, sometimes untested items may not work or may disturb the production routine to the detriment of plan fulfillment. Moreover, the introduction of new technologies may also create new costs and difficulties, requiring training workers, acquiring ancillary equipment and production inputs, and developing a new network of suppliers and customers.[18]

China's decision in the early 1950s to replicate the Soviet model imposed a set of similar constraints on China's innovation capabilities. In particular, like the USSR, the Chinese were faced with the problem of how to generate technological change through primary reliance on a high centralized administrative apparatus. The general absence of market-like incentives from within the Chinese industrial system meant that most of the research and development activities undertaken were also the result of a top-down process of decision-making and project selection.

This tendency to favor a top-down "technology-push" approach to innovation was first reflected in the twelve-year science and technology plan announced in 1956. The plan, which was designed to catapult China into the forefront of the industrialized nations, identified twelve technology areas that were closely linked to the building of a strong, vibrant economy and a modern defense capability. For example, radio electronics and computers, automation, metallurgy, and heavy machinery were among the designated priority fields. The influence of the Soviet Union was quite strong throughout the 1950s. The USSR furnished China with the equipment and know-how for 156 major industrial projects. Furthermore, Soviet engineers and industrial designers made considerable contributions to China's research and development efforts. As such, most of the Chinese innovation-related programs were imitative, relying extensively on Soviet blueprints, designs, standards, and specifications.[19]

The Soviet Union also had a major influence on the structure of the Chinese S&T system. Its advice resulted in the formalization of a rather explicit division of labor in the research sector and economy. Three major organizational structures for science and technology activities were delineated: (1) the Chinese Academy of Sciences (CAS), which housed China's basic research institutes; (2) the industrial ministries, which became the supposed home for applied research institutes, including the military; and (3) the universities, which, for the most part, focused on training rather than research.[20] Out of this three-legged structure emerged a highly vertical, compartmented research system. Each of the individual branches tended to behave in a very insular fashion, with limited mechanisms for horizontal interaction with their counterparts. Consequently, research activities were rarely coordinated (except from above), projects were often duplicated, and existing resources frequently went underutilized.

The CAS, which was reorganized along the lines of its Soviet counterpart, illustrates the type of problems encountered within the evolving system. As Genevieve Dean has noted, "the government's strategy was to focus the Academy's resources on advanced technical problems rather than on [general economic] modernization, which could be accomplished through imports and existing technologies."[21] This had the result of reinforcing the separation of the institutes under the Academy from the economy. Yet, while the Academy was considered to be the vanguard of basic research in China, it was also ostracised for making little practical contribution to the goals of national economic construction.[22] The CAS's problems in this regard reflected a basic structural dilemma that still exists. On the one hand, the CAS had been mandated to assume a position of leadership in China's research system; on the other hand, it was confronted with numerous pressures to solve a host of practical technical problems. Despite the preferences of many scientists in the Academy, these problems could not be ignored in view of the prevailing dearth of scientific and technical personnel *and* specialized equipment in China. It became clear that additional resources would be needed to handle the tasks of industrial R&D.

The imperative of ensuring that research and engineering support would be available to Chinese industry resulted in the steady albeit gradual development of an R&D capability under China's industrial ministries, at the central level, and the provincial and municipal industrial bureaus, at the local level. As indicated earlier, this system was initially oriented toward the replication of Soviet designs and technologies. Gradually, however, as it became clear that dependence on the USSR was becoming excessive, the Chinese sought to establish a more independent R&D capability, one based on a set of indigenous institutions able to develop their own models and introduce their own innovations.[23] The Soviet Union's pullout in 1960 advanced the pace of this effort, as the Chinese were faced with the difficult task of completing many of the projects that had been abandoned by Soviet technicians.[24] As Rawski has noted, this experience of "regrouping available resources" to cope with unforeseen problems (such as the Soviet departure) helped equip the Chinese with some of the necessary experience to innovate in the future.[25]

As the S&T system became more complex and multifaceted, the need for a different form of administrative control also became evident. By the mid-1950s, as Suttmeier notes, the non-CAS sectors of the S&T system received a greater share of the responsibility and resources for conducting research.[26] Accordingly, it became clear that the CAS could no longer be charged with the task of managing the country's entire S&T effort. In 1956, the CAS was supplanted in the policy-making hierarchy by two central administrative bodies, the State Technological Commission and the Science Planning Commission, which in 1958 were merged into the State Science and Technology Commission (SSTC).[27] The SSTC became the nation's leading organization for S&T policy. Although it did not engage in any research on its own and was staffed principally by nonscientists—which still chagrins many CAS personnel—the SSTC was also made responsible for overseeing the design and implementation of the country's R&D efforts both inside and outside the CAS, which included the promotion of industrial innovation. In theory, therefore, the commission was placed in the pivotal position of providing an organizational link for the many separate entities engaged in research and development.

Despite the centralization of responsibility for research in the SSTC, the Maoist leadership of the period also strongly encouraged mass involvement in science and technology activities. This is probably one of the biggest differences between China and the Soviet Union. At the time of China's Great Leap Forward in 1958, for example, added emphasis was given to a "bottom-up" style of innovation behavior, one that viewed technological development as the product of the ingenuity and labors of the masses rather than the result of traditional forms of scientific practice and discovery.[28] At issue was the question of "red" versus "expert," a debate that centered on the role of politics in all endeavors, including research. After the failure of the Great Leap in 1960, the attention given to the role of "mass" innovation greatly diminished, but the issue would emerge again during the Cultural Revolution, when China's scientists and technically trained personnel were vilified and subjected to political criticism.

The Great Leap Forward also raised another significant issue, namely the extent to which the primary impetus for innovative activities should reside at the local or national level. Through its emphasis on greater decentralization of authority and local self-reliance, the Great Leap helped to stimulate the development of a fully articulated local S&T system, including provincial and municipal counterparts to the SSTC and a vast network of local research institutes. As Hans Heymann notes, the existence of this local R&D sector allowed "local government authorities to engage in a great deal of pragmatic innovation and improvisation, to organize cooperative technological ventures, to integrate the scientific and productive forces of the local area and to mobilize them toward the fulfillment of local or national tasks."[29] Yet, while the emergence of this local R&D sector did bring research units into closer proximity with potential end-users, especially in the case of rural industry, it also served to exacerbate many of the coordination and duplication problems that plagued the system at the central level. Moreover, in Beijing the local sector was always viewed as the poor cousin to the centrally controlled units. This reinforced some of the problems of regionalism that have characterized China's bureaucratic system since traditional times.

To understand the process of innovation within the system described above, it is essential to examine the relationship between China's industrial structure and its research organizations. As in the USSR, the majority of China's research institutes were neither physically or administratively linked to production enterprises. Most medium and large enterprises did have internal "engineering or design" departments, but, as their name implies, these were not traditional research entities. Aside from in the military, end-user involvement in the structuring of an institute's research portfolio or selection of research priorities was extremely limited. Similarly, research institutes hardly ever consulted with factory managers regarding their research agenda or possible collaboration. This situation prevailed not only because of the vertical and highly compartmented character of the system, but also because of the ways funds for R&D were allocated to institutes and factories *and* because of the incentive structure that drove enterprise behavior.

We can distinguish three main categories of funding for R&D in support of innovation activities. First, one group of funds were destined for use in new capital construction (*jiben jianshe*), including fixed capital investments such as new facilities and large machinery. A second group of funds were allocated to support "technical transformation" (*jishu gaizao*). This category would include facility updating and upgrading, equipment replacement or modification, and improvements in operating efficiency, such as the application of an energy savings device. The third group of funds was designated to support directly research, design, and engineering activities. In contrast to the other two types of expenditures, this pool of funds, known as *san xiang feiyong* (three expenditures), was more closely tied to the actual innovation effort. More specifically, these funds supported the development of new products, the trial production of new products, and the dissemination of new products and processes.

The bulk of these funds were allocated in a highly centralized and planned fashion. Research institutes dispersed the various budgetary allocations they received in the form of grants, without any consideration for group performance or individual scientific and technological achievement. Moreover, research results, if they were transferred to enterprises, were delivered gratis, since China did not have a patent law (until April 1985) and did not accept the notion of privatization of knowledge. Ideas and know-how, therefore, moved by administrative fiat and had little relationship to commercial processes. With funding basically guaranteed each year, researchers had little concern about whether the results of their labor could be translated into production. Here again, the system worked best in areas such as the military where China's command-like administrative structure would actively assert itself to ensure that national priorities were given adequate attention. For the most part, however, the funding patterns supported a system where innovative performance and budgetary decisions were disassociated from one another, resulting in the creation and preservation of the so-called "iron rice bowl" within the research community.

On the production side, a percentage of the operating budgets allocated to the respective industrial ministries was set aside each year to support industrial R&D activities. Specific projects proposed by either research institutes or production enterprises were selected in response to the guidance plans that were announced by the central government. These plans, which were formulated by experts from all around the country, also reflected the predispositions of the industrial ministries and their enterprises that, in general, had been communicated to the central organs through both formal and informal channels.[30] Complementing this funding procedure, there was a sizable budget set aside by the central and provincial/municipal governments for funding special national or local priority projects on a sustained basis. Each year, several hundred projects were designated in this category, and as such, the project recipients (which were organizations and not individuals) received financial support above and beyond the monies already appropriated to the ministries for support of general R&D activities.

Yet, while monies were made available to the industrial system, the emphasis on attainment of state-set quotas made for risk-averse enterprise managers and chief engineers that were generally oriented away from investing funds into innovation activities. Dean describes this orientation:

> It was not the cost of experimental development but rather the risk to production that deterred the chief engineer from introducing innovation. From management's point of view, any experimentation that involved production facilities was a risk to output and to fulfillment of production quotas in the state plan. Pressure to meet production quotas even caused management to avoid the trial-production assignments that were included in the state plan, were accompanied by allocations of state funds to cover the additional costs involved, and for which adjustment could be made in the enterprise's production plan.[31]

Aside from the research activities associated with the aforementioned priority projects, much of the so-called research that did take place within enterprises was of a troubleshooting or problem-solving nature. In these cases, given their almost Edisonian character, it would be difficult to call these efforts a full-fledged program for industrial or technological innovation. Moreover, even when innovative opportunities were pursued, support from higher authorities in the industrial sector was often lacking. These "economic" organizations usually lacked well-developed working ties with their counterparts in the science and technology policy field. In addition, as Rudi Volti notes, "technological changes required the approval of central agencies," and since these changes could upset the prevailing production system, such agencies were often reluctant to approve them.[32]

In essence, China relied on the planning mechanism as the principal instrument for promoting greater innovation and R&D. As Marianne Bastid suggests in discussing the levels of decision making in the economy, "in practice, local initiative [was] allowed to operate [but] only within the framework of a directive or plan received from above, with no encroachment, at least in the early stage, on the set pattern for the allocation of funds and resources and without prejudice to the regular procurements already assigned to the units concerned."[33] A number of barriers existed, however, that did limit the quality and quantity of innovative activities. Nonetheless, the use of a centralized administrative apparatus to foster innovation did have its benefits, particularly in the areas of national defense. Responsibility for managing the country's defense-related R&D was placed in the hands of the National Defense Science and Technology Commission. This, like the SSTC, its counterpart on the civilian side, managed and directed all defense R&D efforts. Its activities were complemented in the production area by the National Defense Industries Office (NDIO), which handled all military-related manufacturing. To accomplish their mission, these two organizations relied on a number of fully dedicated industrial institutes and factories under the so-called machine-building ministries. They were also able to enlist help from organizations such as the CAS and scientists in the university sector.

On paper, however, military research and production were also institutionally separated. That China has been able to bring about sustained integration between the two when needed is an exceptional achievement. In contrast to the general situation in the civilian sector, where the problems of coordination and cooperation were pervasive, high-level Party and military officials in Beijing were able to task and mobilize specialized personnel and physical resources to work on high-priority projects. This often involved creating special teams of scientists and engineers, such as was the case in China's atomic and hydrogen bomb programs.

Yet the Chinese military was not invincible in its ability to innovate. Research efforts were difficult to sustain and coordinate, and collaboration, particularly with civilian organizations, was usually quite problematic due to extremely tight national security compartmentation. Political infighting also affected the nature of the research environment.[34] In addition, the 1960s decision to move into remote areas a substantial portion of their defense industrial and R&D units, i.e. third line industries, for national security reasons created tremendous communication problems as well as physical barriers to any type of sustained interaction. This caused the military severe problems in its overall R&D performance. While they may not have prevented China from developing a substantial military capability, these problems were serious enough to limit the pace and full extent of technological advance in comparison with the United States and the USSR. Moreover, despite the continued tendency today of some Chinese leaders to seek out ways to replicate this experience, questions remain whether it can be duplicated given the extent of recent changes.

INNOVATION AND THE CULTURAL REVOLUTION

The Chinese approach to the problems of innovation generation contained all of the trappings of the Soviet-style command structure. However, this encrusted Soviet model of research and innovation was periodically shaken up by Mao's own vision of scientific and technological development, specifically during the Greap Leap Forward from 1958 to 1960 and the Cultural Revolution. Over time, a number of fundamental issues emerged that led to a questioning of several facets of the Soviet model. Most important, China was still a developing country, with all of the associated problems. With a shortage of investment capital and necessary personnel and resources, it was initially assumed that a centralized system would be the answer to China's need for a technological and economic takeoff. However, as the economy and R&D system evolved, dissatisfaction with their character appeared among some of the more radical political elements in the Party and government. Given their strong dislike for the growing power and influence of China's scientific elite and technical professionals during the early 1960s, these persons felt that a radically different approach to the problems of science and technology development was needed.

In effect, neither the Soviet nor the Western models would be appropriate for China. Accordingly, a major debate arose over such matters as the correct sources of innovation, the role of science and technology in society, the management of R&D, and the degree of central versus local control. The upshot of this debate was the launching of the Cultural Revolution (GPCR). While it is not our purpose to enter into a long, extended discussion of this event, it is important to note that the GPCR had a major impact on the nature of the innovation process.

At the time of this movement in China, many in the West heralded the GPCR because as a grassroots movement, it placed more emphasis on people than machines and rejected a pattern of societal development where technocratic and scientific elites controlled the reins of power. Politics was in command, which meant that the "instruments of technical management and control [were adjusted] to realize different policy objectives."[35] These objectives included a shift away from a development model where the primary impetus for innovation was in the hands of a highly centralized bureaucracy or those supporting it. As Dean notes, more emphasis was placed on the role of the worker as the primary source of innovation.

> . . . after the start of the Cultural Revolution, the Chinese press was reporting numerous successful "worker-innovations", which were usually represented as the outcome of a conflict between management and the workers. Management, it was claimed, had suppressed workers' proposals for improving current technologies, in order to strengthen its claims for new capital allocations from the state. The workers, on the other hand, contributed to the "self-reliance" of the enterprise by increasing output without such requisitions, thus saving state resources for investment in new construction and "expanded production".[36]

In essence, during the Cultural Revolution, Mao imposed his, rather than the Soviet Union's, social and political criteria onto technological and economic activities. He emphasized mass participation, egalitarianism, self-reliance, and indigenous scientific and technological development. Party cadres and representatives of the masses were to take over technological and scientific tasks from the professionals, who were criticized for their "ivory tower" mentality and sent to the countryside or to factories to learn from the masses. Campaigns involving political mobilization and ideological exhortation rather than scientific study and laboratory experiments were supposed to achieve desired technological breakthroughs. And, in fact, whether due to the inspiration of Mao's thought or not, a wide variety of technological achievements were made during these periods of political turbulence. For example, through the establishment of the 3-in-1 combinations (cadres, experts, and masses) in research and the formation of small neighborhood factories and research units, large quantities of waste materials were transformed into useful products—candles, screws, soap, and fertilizer.[37]

The Cultural Revolution did loosen the rigidity and narrowness of the Soviet-style system. Nonetheless, it also severely damaged rather than advanced China's scientific and technological development. The central planning apparatus responsible for implementing China's S&T development was disrupted, and power devolved to worker- and peasant-run institutes and ministries. This resulted in even less productivity than before. Without strong support from a technical contingent, and lacking modern equipment, organizational innovations such as the 3-in-1 combinations could not sustain a high-quality research program. While new products such as integrated circuits and computers were being developed and manufactured, the performance and reliability of an appreciable percentage of these items were severely lacking.

Even more damaging were the political campaigns which not only closed Chinese universities, but also demoralized and decimated several generations of scientists who had been trained in the West and the Soviet Union. As the movement gained momentum, the Cultural Revolution swept up virtually all intellectuals, including scientists. The exceptions were a small number working on weapons development, though recent evidence indicates that even these individuals were not immune from attack. All formal academic and scientific research work was stopped as scientists and engineers were re-educated and sent for "thought reform" in the countryside and factories. When a small number of universities and research institutes were reopened in the early 1970s, they still used political rather than scientific criteria to carry on their work. As Chinese leaders were to discover when they sought to resurrect the S&T system after the fall of the Gang of Four in 1976, the damage that had been done to the country's modest S&T infrastructure would take years to repair.

RETHINKING A RETURN TO THE SOVIET-STYLE MODEL

Since the formal inception of the four modernizations program in February 1978, Chinese leaders have continued to attach great importance to S&T modernization and improved R&D performance.[38] Although "science and technology" were listed as number three in the hierarchy of modernization priorities, in fact, Chinese leaders recognize that progress in science and technology is a basic prerequisite to more rapid and sustained growth in industry, agriculture, and national defense.[39] The pivotal role to be played by science and technology was most clearly articulated at the time of the March 1978 National Science Conference, when China's highest political and scientific leaders noted that "the crux of the four modernizations rests with science and technology development."[40]

The National Science Conference signified the importance that the regime attached to improvements in both research and education.[41] The comprehensive program announced at the March meeting had been the product of many months of intensive political discussion and negotiation that had begun as early as late 1976. China's stated goal was to catch up with the advanced nations in science and technology by the year 2000. In much the same way as the twelve-year S&T plan in 1956, a set of eight priority areas were spelled out for immediate attention. It becomes readily apparent after looking at the list of priorities that their selection reflected not one homogeneous viewpoint, but the varying interests of the different institutional groups concerned with science and technology modernization.

The remarkable result of the National Science Conference was that basic research was allowed to command significant amounts of financial and personnel resources—both of which had been in short supply. This is not to suggest that applied research and industrial innovation were totally ignored. However, it did signal the strong influence of the CAS in the formulation and implementation of science and technology policy. It also brought to the surface the continued disinterest and, in some cases, reluctance of the industrial sector to seize upon the new opportunities for product and process improvement that were being made available as a result of the new emphasis being given to S&T. Thus it suggested that the key to expanded interest in industrial innovation and a more responsive research establishment would not necessarily *only* come from the center itself. Rather, a new set of operating principles and mechanisms was needed to manage technology affairs. The catalyst for bringing about more relevant results and products from the innovation process was to be found elsewhere in the system.[42]

Interestingly, however, an important dimension of the 1978 national science plan was the lack of attention paid to reform of the basic structure and design of the domestic S&T system itself. After the downfall of the Gang of Four, Chinese leaders basically tried to rehabilitate the system as it existed prior to the Cultural Revolution rather than considering fundamental structural change. At the height of the Cultural Revolution, the SSTC had been disbanded and replaced by a revolutionary committee charged with overseeing science and technology affairs. In 1977, however, re-establishment of the SSTC was one of the first steps taken by the Deng-led regime as it attempted to revitalize the country's traumatized research sector. Moreover, very little was done to alter the situation in the university sector regarding the harnessing of scientific personnel for research purposes. In the view of many Chinese administrators and scientists, some of whom had received extensive training in the Soviet Union, the Soviet-style system had produced nuclear weapons and other desired scientific and technological advances, and was therefore not an obvious obstacle to innovation.

The initial response to the new stress placed on technology modernization was mixed, resulting in wide variations in the ways in which policies formulated in Beijing were interpreted throughout the country and within each research institute and industrial enterprise. In some localities, local cadres and managers within various institutes and factories ignored or paid only lip service to the call for new products and processes. As pointed out at a December 1979 national forum on progress in science and technology, "quite a few leading cadres were still accustomed to giving guidance to scientific and technological work by adopting the method of promoting political movements."[43] Moreover, unwilling to relinquish their political positions, they obstructed the call for placing persons with technical credentials in positions of authority. Their behavior was primarily motivated by two factors—self-interest, and an apprehension that the political winds might once again shift and that a high-profile pro-science position might turn out to be politically dangerous.

Although the majority of scientific and technical personnel received China's renewed emphasis on technology and innovation in a positive way, a large percentage remained skeptical about the staying power of the new leadership and its policies. Some scientists, fearful of once again being singled out for pursuing their intellectual activities or engaging in a research "failure," received the statements coming out of Beijing with some trepidation.[44] In many instances, this led to widespread duplication of research already done abroad, particularly regarding "successful" projects that had been completed in the West or other parts of China. It was politically safer to undertake and repeat a proven research experiment than to assume responsibility for a more speculative venture.

In other instances, there was a bandwagon response to Beijing's emphasis on industrial innovation. Many local officials, some sincere in their efforts to dispel the disdain for technology that had been engendered by the Cultural Revolution and others anxious to court Beijing's favor, went to extremes in popularizing the value of S&T to peasants and workers. The movement to popularize science and technology led to a massive outflow of rather simplistic "scientific and technical publications" and to a proliferation of relatively worthless research institutes. In one province, the number of these institutes increased by 153 percent in one year. Many of these institutes came to be called the three no centers—having no projects, no equipment, and no personnel. In other areas, as noted above, the stress on popularizing and engaging in science and technology led to extensive attempts to replicate foreign research, much having little practical or immediate value to China's needs. The tendency to pursue S&T activities in such a fashion was reinforced by the rapidity with which China was expanding its S&T contacts with the outside world. In many cases, the development of these contacts forced China to try to give the appearance of engaging in world-class research.

The difficulties encountered within the realm of the research system itself were compounded by Chinese behavior regarding the acquisition of foreign technology and equipment.[45] Here again, the general response to the announcement of the "four modernizations" was to proceed as in the past, with primary emphasis given to the purchase of whole plants and equipment rather than actual technology and know-how. Articles appearing in the Chinese press have suggested that less than 10 percent of the funds expended for so-called technology imports actually went for technology.[46] Numerous delegations and buying missions were sent abroad to survey the state of the art in various fields. Many of these missions signed contracts for advanced items which China could not possibly use.

Other contracts were signed by over-enthusiastic technical delegations which in fact had little authority to commit scarce Chinese foreign exchange for these purchases. In most cases, feasibility studies and project assessments were not conducted beforehand, resulting in inefficient use of both imported items and domestic resources. For example, most of the ancillary equipment and infrastructure needed to make the whole plant and equipment purchases worthwhile were lacking. As in the case of the Baoshan steel mill, the results were disastrous, with very little actual technology transfer taking place.

Although many of these problems had begun to surface by the time of the Third Plenum in December 1978, it was not until early 1981 when they assumed a leading position on the working agenda of the top leadership. During the period after the Third Plenum, many of the expectations that earlier had been placed on the efficacy of the research system for generating technological innovation disappeared. The program of readjustment that was announed at the Third Plenum, embodied in the so-called eight-character slogan of "readjustment, restructuring, consolidation and improvement," consumed the full attention of both economic and political leaders. At the Second and Third Sessions of the Fifth National People's Congress (June 1979 and September 1980, respectively), several large projects were cut back and researchers were encouraged to assist with the economic modernization program. From an overall perspective, however, the critical shortcomings of the research system were addressed only implicitly. Not until the signals underlying economic behavior were rectified could Beijing expect a change in attitudes and actions regarding innovation.

In early 1981, a major revision of the approach for stimulating innovation and promoting S&T advance was introduced. This new approach was reflected in the Xinhua (official Chinese news agency) admonition that "in performing science and technology work, we should make the promotion of economic development our primary task."[47]

The full thrust of the new approach was described in two interviews, one with Yang Jike, former vice-governor of Anhui and a member of the faculty at the Chinese University of Science and Technology, and the other with Tong Dalin, former vice-minister of the SSTC. According to Yang, "the past practice of devoting much manpower and money to isolated sophisticated topics without regard for economic results must change."[48] Tong highlighted five new principles to guide all science and technology work:

1. S&T will be coordinated with the growth of the economy.
2. Production technologies and their application will be the key focus of research activity.
3. Enterprises should expand their research efforts and strive to popularize research fundings.
4. Continued efforts should be made at studying foreign S&T developments.
5. Basic research should not be ignored, but should grow at a steady, but gradual pace.[49]

The new policy was most fully expressed in a *Peoples Daily* editorial on April 7, 1981.[50] Summarizing further the results of the December 1980 S&T meeting, the editorial noted that the time has come to move away from only "paying attention to advanced science and technology, ignoring production, and reaching for what is beyond one's grasp and of blindly catching up with and surpassing others." The editorial suggested two reasons to account for China's poor performance in developing key production technologies: a lack of competition that has fostered a disregard for economic results and the tendency to rely principally on increased capital construction rather than new technology to expand production output.

A more severe criticism of ongoing practices within the R&D sector was presented in another editorial in the Shanghai-based *Liberation Daily* in June 1981.[51] The article, which blamed many of China's problems in the R&D realm on the continued influence of leftist elements, pointed to five problems that had affected China's climate for innovation:

1. Placing too much emphasis on blindly catching up with the West
2. Failure to pay adequate attention to the quality of research
3. Impatience for success
4. Continued duplication of research
5. Neglecting the links between science and technology and the economy

The last problem, however, continued to be the key to what both economic planners and S&T administrators believed was the real failure of Chinese science and technology modernization efforts—a primary cause of which was the lack of formal institutional linkages between those responsible for determining economic needs and objectives and those responsible for setting research priorities.

NOTES

1. Nancy Dorfman, *Innovation and Market Structure: Lessons from the Computer and Semiconductor Industries* (Cambridge, Mass.: Ballinger, 1987), p. 32.
2. Alec Nove, *Socialism, Economics and Development* (London: Allen & Unwin, 1986), pp. 49–190.

3. Ronald Amann, Julian Cooper, and Robert Davies, ed., *The Technological Level of Soviet Industry* (New Haven: Yale University Press, 1977).

4. Edward Roberts, ed., *Generating Technological Innovation* (New York: Oxford University Press, 1987), pp. 3–21.

5. Devendra Sahal, *Patterns of Technological Innovation* (Reading, Mass.: Addison-Wesley, 1981), pp. 41–45.

6. National Science Foundation, *The Process of Technological Innovation: Reviewing the Literature* (Washington, D.C.: National Science Foundation, 1983).

7. Daniel Roman and Joseph Puett, *International Business and Technological Innovation* (New York: North-Holland, 1983), pp. 249–278.

8. James Utterback, "The Dynamics of Product and Process Innovation in Industry," in Christopher Hill and James Utterback, eds., *Technological Innovation for a Dynamic Economy* (New York: Pergamon Press, 1979), pp. 42–65.

9. Bruce Parrott, *Politics and Technology in the Soviet Union* (Cambridge, Mass.: MIT Press, 1983).

10. Robert Burgelman and Modesto Maidique, *Strategic Management of Technology and Innovation* (Homewood, Ill.: Irwin Publishers, 1988), pp. 34–44.

11. Joseph Schumpeter, *Capitalism, Socialism and Democracy* (London: Allen & Unwin, 1966).

12. Ronald Amann and Julian Cooper, eds., *Industrial Innovation in the Soviet Union* (New Haven: Yale University Press, 1982).

13. Edwin Mansfield et al., *Technology Transfer, Productivity and Economic Policy* (New York: Norton and Company, 1982), pp. 27–49.

14. Charles Stewart and Yasumitsu Nihei, *Technology Transfer and Human Factors* (Lexington, Mass.: Lexington Books, 1987), pp. 1–35.

15. Peter Solomon, "Technological Innovation and Soviet Industrialization," in Mark Field, ed., *Social Consequences of Modernization in Communist Societies* (Baltimore: Johns Hopkins University Press, 1976), pp. 207–233.

16. Joseph Berliner, *The Innovation Decision in Soviet Industry* (Cambridge, Mass.: MIT Press, 1976), pp. 98–99.

17. Ronald Amann and Julian Cooper, eds., *Technological Progress and Soviet Economic Development* (London: Blackwell, 1986), p. 16.

18. William J. Conyngham, *The Modernization of Soviet Industrial Management* (Cambridge: Cambridge University Press, 1982), pp. 32–37.

19. Genevieve Dean, *Technology Policy and Industrialization in the People's Republic of China* (Ottawa: International Development Research Center, 1979), pp. 23–34.

20. The Chinese usually refer to their S&T system as having five primary components: (1) the institutes under the Chinese Academy of Sciences; (2) the research institutes under the industrial ministries; (3) the university-based research institutes; (4) the military-dedicated research units; and (5) the institutes at the provincial and municipal level.

21. Dean, *Technology Policy and Industrialization in the People's Republic of China*, p. 29.

22. Denis Fred Simon, "China's Scientists and Technologists in the Post-Mao Era: A Retrospective and Prospective Glimpse," in Merle Goldman, ed., *China's Intellectuals and the State: In Search of a New Relationship* (Cambridge, Mass.: Harvard University Press, 1987), pp. 129–136.

23. Dean, *Technology Policy and Industrialization in the People's Republic of China*, pp. 32–36.

24. Harry Gelber, *Technology, Defense, and External Relations in China, 1975–78* (Boulder, Colo.: Westview Press, 1979), pp. 141–147.

25. Thomas Rawski, *China's Transition to Industrialism* (Ann Arbor, Mich.: University of Michigan Press, 1980), pp. 70–81.

26. Richard P. Suttmeier, *Research and Revolution: Science Policy and Societal Change in China* (Lexington, Mass.: Lexington Books, 1974), pp. 47–78.

27. Ibid., p. 66.

28. Rudi Volti, *Technology, Politics, and Society in China* (Boulder, Colo.: Westview Press, 1982), pp. 36–46.

29. Hans Heymann, "Industrial Structure and Technological Advancement," in Organization for Economic Cooperation and Development, ed., *Science and Technology in the People's Republic of China* (Paris: OECD, 1976), p. 231.

30. William Fischer, "Scientific and Technical Planning in the People's Republic of China," *Technological Forecasting and Social Change 25*, no. 3 (May 1984): 189–207.

31. Dean, *Technology Policy and Industrialization*, p. 58.

32. Volti, *Technology, Politics, and Society in China*, pp. 105–110.

33. Marianne Bastid, "Levels of Economic Decision-making," in Stuart Schram, ed., *Authority, Participation and Cultural Change in China* (Cambridge: Cambridge University Press, 1973), pp. 193–194.

34. Ellis Joffe, *The Chinese Army After Mao* (Cambridge, Mass.: Harvard University Press, 1987).

35. Dean, *Technology Policy and Industrialization*, p. 85.

36. Genevieve Dean, "Research and Technological Innovation in Industry," in Organization for Economic Cooperation and Development, ed., *Science and Technology in the People's Republic of China* (Paris: OECD, 1976), p. 260.

37. Leo Orleans, "China's Science and Technology: Continuity and Innovation," in U.S. Congress, Joint Economic Committee, *People's Republic*

of China: An Economic Assessment (Washington, D.C.: U.S. Government Printing Office, 1972), pp. 207–213.

38. Denis Fred Simon, "Implementing China's S&T Modernization Program," in David Michael Lampton, ed., *Policy Implementation in Post-Mao China* (Berkeley: University of California Press, 1987), pp. 354–379.

39. Richard Baum, ed. *China's Four Modernizations* (Boulder, Colo.: Westview Press, 1980).

40. Richard P. Suttmeier, *Science, Technology and China's Drive for Modernization* (Stanford, Calif.: Hoover Institution Press, 1980).

41. Jon Sigurdson, *Technology and Science in the People's Republic of China: An Introduction* (New York: Pergamon, 1980).

42. Simon, "Implementing China's S&T Modernization Program."

43. "National Scientific and Technological Conference in Beijing," *Foreign Broadcast Information Service—People's Republic of China,* December 6, 1979, p. L11.

44. A forum on scientific achievement was held in Beijing in December 1980 to discuss the procedures for appraising scientific work. A large degree of concern was expressed about continued "administrative interference" in academic issues, reflecting the apprehensions of many scientists. According to one of the conference participants, although many scientists have been rehabilitated, "the historical and social origins of [previous] problems have yet to be earnestly analyzed. We have not learned lessons from this matter." See "Forum on Scientific Achievement Held in Beijing," *Foreign Broadcast Information Service—People's Republic of China,* December 22, 1980, p. L40.

45. Denis Fred Simon, "China's Capacity to Assimilate Foreign Technology: An Assessment," in U.S. Congress, Joint Economic Committee, *China Under the Four Modernizations* (Washington, D.C.: U.S. Government Printing Office, 1982), pp. 514–552.

46. Yang Haitian, "Position in International Technology Transfer Discussed," translated in *Joint Publications Research Service 80736,* May 5, 1982.

47. "Beijing Radio Stresses the Use of Science in the Economy," in *Joint Publications Research Service, China Examines Science Policy* (Washington, D.C.: Joint Publications Research Service, 1982), pp. 1–2.

48. "Renmin Ribao: Applied Science to be Emphasized," Xinhua News Agency, January 29, 1981, translated in *Foreign Broadcast Information Service,* February 5, 1981, pp. L8–9.

49. "Xinhua Interviews Science and Technology Official," in *Joint Publications Research Service, China Examines Science Policy,* January 1982, p. 11.

50. "Further Clarify the Policy for the Development of Science and Technology," in *Renmin Ribao,* April 7, 1981, p. 1, translated in *Joint Publications Research Service, China Examines Science Policy,* January 1982, pp. 16–19.

51. Xia Yulong and Liu Ji, "It Is Also Necessary to Eliminate Erroneous Leftist Influence in the Science and Technology Front," *Jiefang Ribao* (Liberation Daily), Shanghai, June 2, 1981, p. 1.

2 CHINA'S INDUSTRIAL AND TECHNOLOGY STRATEGY

Whether or not the numerous problems confronting our economic construction can be effectively resolved depends on whether or not major breakthroughs can be achieved in scientific and technological areas. Similarly whether or not our economic development can keep forging ahead also depends on the most profound source of stamina, namely scientific and technological development.

—Premier Zhao Ziyang
March 25, 1986

Chinese leaders are still faced with a backward and generally inefficient domestic science and technology system. Since the early 1980s, they have been engaged in an all-out effort to restructure their research sector and to modernize indigenous S&T capabilities. This effort has undergone a number of significant changes in focus and direction since its resurgence in early 1978. Nonetheless, a number of themes have remained constant; the most outstanding is the drive to improve the links between research and production. The roots of this drive go back to the twelve-year S&T plan discussed in the previous chapter. The Chinese leadership recognizes that without significant contributions by the S&T sector to industry, agriculture, and national defense, it will be hard to sustain the long-term momentum of their modernization program and to attain their goal of quadrupling the gross value of industrial and agricultural output by the year 2000.

25

In contrast to the regime's initial efforts to promote scientific and technological advance in the aftermath of the March 1978 National Science Conference, the current drive strongly emphasizes organizational reform and structural change in the R&D system. So far, the reforms proposed in science and technology have been extensive. The degree to which the leadership is prepared to initiate fundamental change is exemplified by the March 1985 Central Committee Decision on Reforms in Science and Technology. The document spells out a broad array of modifications regarding the funding of science and technology activities as well as the treatment of technical know-how and the procedures for managing scientific and technical personnel. Most important, the document attempts to make explicit the role and responsibilities of government actors (central and local), research institutes, and production enterprises in science and technology work. By helping to clarify these roles, the Chinese leadership is hoping to break down the bureaucratic boundaries and related obstacles that have long worked against the effective and efficient use of S&T resources.

China's current efforts to reform its S&T system must be viewed against the backdrop of the ongoing efforts in two contexts: other socialist systems; and both the industrialized nations and the Third World. China's attempt to find a more successful formula to promote technological innovation and advance has parallels in both cases—with the functions of government being redefined so that it can play more of a facilitative role. China's policy of introducing so-called market forces as a tool for managing its economy and stimulating technological advance, while at the same time still relying on centrally directed control over research in key areas, stands out as one attempt to sort out the most appropriate strategy for promoting innovation in the research sector. In many respects, the Chinese two-pronged strategy is a unique experiment. There are numerous historical examples in both the East and West that suggest the presence of inherently contradictory elements in such a strategy.[1] Nonetheless, Chinese leaders appear committed to the simultaneous use of what Lindblom has called "authority structures" and "exchange mechanisms" to promote national scientific and technological modernization.[2]

Underlying China's emerging science and technology strategy is a two-edged definition of reform. On the one hand, one dimension of S&T reform has focused on initiating improvements in the operation of the existing centrally oriented S&T structure. The desire to maintain the central tasking mechanism reflects two factors. First, as suggested, the leadership continues to look back fondly on some of its previous successes in science and technology, foremost among them the development of atomic weapons and intercontinental ballistic missiles (ICBMs). These achievements were made by the military through a top-down process, with the national defense S&T and production organs working together to mobilize and target the country's limited S&T capabilities on a high-priority project. The decision to appoint Song Jian, formerly affiliated with China's Ministry of Space Industry, as head of the State Science and Technology Commission in 1983 seems to reflect a determination to maintain some aspects of the command system in science and technology affairs. And second, the leadership refuses to allow the vagaries of the market to determine the outcome of future priority endeavors—favoring instead to reserve a number of key technology areas, e.g. large-scale integrated circuits, for nurturing by centrally directed organizations. Accordingly, in 1983 a special leading group for electronics development was created under the State Council to coordinate and manage *national* development of capabilities in this important field.

On the other hand, the complementary side of the S&T reform movement has been focused on the introduction of essentially new operating principles and institutions into the research system.[3] The Chinese leadership recognizes that the key to the postwar development of American technological capabilities and vitality is in a combination of entrepreneurial talent and market stimuli. Nancy Dorfman, for example, in her analysis of the emergence of Route 128 in Massachusetts, suggests that the "electronics boom occurred basically without the benefit of concerted efforts to make it happen by academic institutions, government bodies, or other interest groups."[4] In this context, an explicit attempt has been made to link the economic reforms with the reform of the S&T system. As Deng Xiaoping has noted,

> The new economic structure must be favorable to science and technology advancement, and the new R&D system should, in turn, be conducive to economic growth. The two systems should go hand in hand, and the long drawn out problem of mismatch between the two may be resolved satisfactorily.[5]

Changes in the operating mode and management of the production enterprise are designed to encourage factory directors to pay more attention to the potential value of adopting new technologies—in both process and production.

This chapter examines the role of recent reforms in China's S&T system, specifying the types of changes the Chinese have introduced and the objectives they hope to achieve. It also identifies the limits to S&T reform, some of which remain in the realm of politics and others that are inherent in the nature of China's economic system. The chapter concludes with a comparative section that not only poses questions about China's reform in comparison with the Soviet Union, but, more broadly, in the context of other Third World efforts. It will be argued that Chinese reforms are on the right track in terms of their primary thrust and direction, but also that the entire effort still lacks an adequate degree of institutional support at the level where it matters the most, that is, at the enterprise and institute level. Accordingly, obstructionism remains a serious and continuing problem—particularly in terms of the treatment of scientific and technical personnel—and one that will require further political reforms if the changes introduced by the leadership are to achieve their desired results.

THE ESSENCE OF S&T REFORM

Beijing's drive to reform its S&T system has been a building block effort. The March 1985 Central Committee document represented, in many respects, the formalization of a process of organizational change and institutional refinement that had begun as early as 1981. On a number of occasions, experimental sites were chosen in order to introduce and test new policies and programs. Given the problems left over from the Cultural Revolution and the historical legacy of tension between the Communist Party and the scientific community, the leadership recognized that it would need a broad base of support to carry out its intended reform program on a broad scale. The process of building coalitions, however, has not been limited to securing support in the Party; a number of other constituencies, e.g. the economic planners, have been skeptical of the merits of investing large sums of financial resources in research and giving the S&T community greater political influence and power.

Much has already been written in China about the need to rebuild the S&T system in the aftermath of the damage engendered by the radical policies of the Gang of Four.[6] This literature is focused on the bottlenecks faced by the leadership in its efforts to construct a system that had been left in shambles by the political turmoil of the ten previous years. Just as important, however, is the fact that China's period of S&T stagnation occurred precisely at the time when the industrialized West was making rapid strides in such key technologies as microelectronics and computers. Due to the prevailing shortage of scientific and technical personnel that developed as a result of the closing of research institutes and universities, as well as Chinese research organizations' lack of necessary equipment and instrumentation, much of the work that has needed to be undertaken has not been completed or has gone undone. Growing concerns about the extent of current resource limitations have caused a great deal of apprehension among many top leaders, as the following quote illustrates:

> We must realize . . . that a new technological revolution has been developing rapidly in the world today and that an increasingly large number of countries are focusing their attention on developing science and technology. Under such circumstances, if we fail to adopt correct policies for taking advantage of this opportunity to confront the challenge, the gap between us and the developed countries will not be narrowed, but it will be further widened instead, and the task of catching up with developed countries economically and technologically will become increasingly more difficult.[7]

The S&T reforms that occurred in early 1981 introduced a number of important changes into the research sector. First, an election at the Chinese Academy of Sciences led to the re-emergence of the 400-member Scientific Council as the governing body of that institution. Putting scientists in charge of scientists was an important step in the effort to give the scientific community confidence in the staying power of the four modernizations. Second, an increasing number of individuals with scientific and technical credentials were being placed in positions of authority not only within institutes but also within government offices at the provincial and municipal level. And third, stronger attention was being paid to the links between research and production. Scientists, engineers, and technical personnel were admonished to ensure that research served the needs of the economy. A concerted effort was made to accomplish this last and perhaps most important goal. However, aside from the encouragement at the top, very few, if any, mechanisms existed to facilitate the development of these types of linkages.

Strategically, the clearest evidence that the leadership was dissatisfied with the pace of S&T advance was the speech made by former premier Zhao Ziyang at the October 1982 national science awards meeting in

Beijing.[8] Zhao's speech attacked those who had been obstructing the central government's efforts to launch a concerted drive to develop the country's S&T base. A few months later, a special leading group for science and technology was created under the State Council headed by Zhao Ziyang. This demonstrated the extent to which Zhao's speech reflected a source of deep concern within the upper echelon of the leadership about the need to speed up S&T modernization.[9]

The role of the State Council's leading group cannot be underestimated, for it has helped to spearhead the reform movement within the S&T arena. The decision to create such a group at such a high level can be attributed to several factors.[10] First, the SSTC had revealed itself unable to carry through on a number of the S&T-related policy initiatives directed by the top leadership. For example, the SSTC was essentially unable to mend its relationship with the CAS, which had been strained ever since the creation of the SSTC in the late 1950s. Second, the need to ensure closer integration between research and the economy meant that greater coordination at the highest levels would be necessary, as well as desirable. More specifically, the State Planning, State Economic and State Science and Technology Commissions would all have to work together on a more sustained basis. The leading group was viewed as a means to accomplish this goal. And third, the leading group with Zhao Ziyang in charge was a way at the time, to place the imprimatur of the office of the premier on the drive to modernize science and technology. Without such visible evidence of high level support, it would have been difficult for the S&T modernization effort to gain sufficient momentum.

The mandate of the leading group included five tasks: (1) long-range science and technology planning; (2) formulation of national policy for key S&T areas; (3) coordination of national level S&T efforts as well as central-local S&T relations; (4) the effective allocation of S&T resources; and (5) reform of the S&T system. According to one member of the office of the leading group, "if the SSTC cannot do something, then we step in." For example, a number of S&T organizations have wanted to publish an S&T newspaper, including the SSTC, CAS, and the Ministry of Education. The leading group stepped in and decided that the SSTC would have the sole responsibility for producing this newspaper, hereafter called the *Keji Ribao* (Science and Technology Daily).

The organization of the leading group appears rather interesting. Under Zhao Ziyang sit three deputies: Fang Yi, an adviser to the State Council who also formerly was minister-in-charge of the SSTC and President of the CAS; Song Ping, minister-in-charge of the State Planning

Commission; and Song Jian, minister-in-charge of the SSTC. A second decision-making tier under the three deputies consists of representatives from the CAS; the State Education Commission; the State Economic Commission; the National Defense Science, Technology, and Industries Commission; and the Ministry of Labor and Personnel. The representatives are responsible for making sure that their parent institutions incorporate S&T considerations into their overall activities.

The office of the S&T leading group is directed by Song Jian, who has two deputies. The office is divided into five functional divisions: (1) management systems, responsible for funding mechanisms and oversight of the science foundation (four to five persons); (2) policy research, which examines broad policy issues (four to five persons); (3) coordination, which ensures that the commissions and the ministries are working together on S&T issues (four to five persons); (4) S&T cadres, which focus on the treatment of scientific and technical personnel as well as issues such as labor mobility (four to five persons); (5) comprehensive affairs, the administrative arm of the leading group (six to seven persons). All together, there are about thirty persons attached to the leading group office.

The power of the leading group comes from the influence it exerts through the various commissions. It does not have a budget for project allocation. However, through the State Planning Commission it can ensure that sufficient funds are made available for specific projects and priorities. The leading group for S&T is somewhat different, for example, than its counterpart at the State Council, the leading group for revitalization of the electronics industry. Even though in principle the two groups share the common goal of improving coordination and bringing greater coherence to key national policy-making areas, the latter group is much more oriented towards substantive issues. The electronics leading group, through a number of formal advisory bodies, helps set electronics and computer policy, whereas the S&T leading group is much more administratively oriented.[11]

Acknowledging this, however, members of the office of the leading group were intimately involved in the drafting of the March 1985 S&T reform document—which in many ways represents the institutionalization of a new approach to managing S&T affairs. In this context, its principal role was ensuring that the substantive recommendations made by various advisers and formal participants were viable from the perspective of the key government bodies. Only in this fashion could the reforms have any credibility. Moreover, without the leading group, the catalyst to bring about fundamental reform in science and technology would probably have been lacking. In this context, in March 1986 the leading group has also played a primary role in helping to draft China's "high-technology" program (*baliusuan*) administered by the SSTC.(See Appendix B.)

THE MARCH 1985 REFORMS

The main impetus to the reform of the science and technology system has been a growing belief that managerial deficiencies and organizational bottlenecks—even more than physical inadequacies—were constraining S&T advance. Wu Mingyu, Deputy Director of the State Council Center for Economic, Technological and Social Research and the former vice-minister of the SSTC, has summed up what most proponents of reform believe are the three major shortcomings of China's prereform S&T research system.[12] First, the system relied too heavily on administrative measures and neglected the role of economic levers in managing S&T activities. Second, there has been a tendency to overdevelop independent research institutes while neglecting S&T activities within production enterprises. For example, China now has over 9,300 research institutes, the majority of which are not directly connected with enterprises (5700). By comparison, over 90 percent of Japan's R&D units are directly linked to companies. Third, there has been excessive rigidity in management of S&T personnel. There is very little mobility, as individuals tend to spend their entire careers in one organization.

The formulation of the reform document apparently involved some rather intense political negotiation and compromise.[13] According to one report, the document was amended eleven times! Moreover, it was reviewed personally by Zhao Ziyang and Hu Yaobang (former Party Secretary) on several occasions. In addition, twenty-five Chinese-American scientists were asked to review the document and render their opinions. As will be discussed later on, the issue that stimulated the most controversy was the question of S&T personnel and labor mobility.

The reform document, which is divided into nine sections, actually focuses on four major issues: reform of the funding system; the establishment of technology markets; the strengthening of enterprise capabilities to absorb and explore for new technologies; and the training and career patterns of young and middle-aged scientific and technical personnel.[14] The most wide-ranging aspect of the S&T reforms deals with funding. Essentially, the central government hopes to alter the past practice of supplying almost 99 percent of research funding in the form of grants. Under the guidelines provided in the reform statement, each year the state will reduce the amount of funds it provides institutes for operating expenses. An appreciable percentage of the projects sponsored by the central and local governments will be issued on the basis of competitive tenders and bids. Moreover, research managers and personnel will be encouraged to seek out research projects themselves in enterprises and the market.

That the central government is actually decreasing the amount of funds it will make directly available to research units does not mean that investment in S&T activities will decline.[15] During the Seventh Five Year Plan (1986–90), the leadership has committed itself to increase the funds available for S&T activities at a faster rate than the growth in general financial expenditures. Major national projects as well as the construction of key laboratories and experimental sites will still be funded by the central or local governments. For example, the development of large-scale integrated circuits is considered one of the country's top S&T priorities. These development efforts will receive substantial support from the central government, though some will come in the form of competitive tenders and bids. The same can be said about China's efforts to build Silicon Valley-like high-technology centers in the different parts of the country, including the Beijing and Shanghai/ Wuxi areas.

In addition, a national science foundation has also been established. This fund builds on a number of more modest funding efforts begun over the last three years in the CAS and the State Seismology Bureau. Institutes engaged in basic and some applied research will be able to draw their project funds from the foundation. The only research entities that will be exempt from these rules will be the ones engaged in research activities in public health, basic technological services, standardization, metrology, monitoring and surveying, and information gathering.[16]

Institutes under the CAS also fall within the guidelines of the reform document. Before the reform, the CAS allocated equal amounts of research funds to each affiliated research unit in accordance with the existing functional divisions. Each institute, in turn, distributed these funds to its research groups without distinguishing their capabilities or performance. Problems often emerged, including duplication, extensive delays in dispersement, and insufficient funding. As a result, the CAS has introduced a contract system that will bind each institute to a certain performance level and schedule. In addition, in 1985, the

CAS withheld 17 percent of the operating budget of a number of successful research institutes. These funds were then used to provide support to research units engaged primarily in theoretical research.[17]

These changes in the modes and mechanisms for funding research could not have been introduced without the second element of the reforms, namely the introduction of so-called technology markets. The decision to treat technology as a commercial commodity represents an abrupt departure from previous thinking, which treated the product of mental labor as a public good that could not be privatized. With the growing support for a national patent law and the realization that technology does have commercial value, the Chinese have tried to stimulate the diffusion of technology through profit-type incentives. Chinese leaders see technology markets playing a variety of roles: stimulate production-oriented research and development; speed up the development time for new products; help delineate research priorities; break down administrative barriers; reward hard work; encourage S&T labor mobility; and improve the status of experts.[18]

Technology markets are viewed as an effective means to help convert research results into production. The first national S&T fair was held in Beijing in 1985 (240 local fairs were held in 1984 and 1985). A total of 4180 actual transactions were made at the fair, with an assessed value of over 2.1 billion yuan. In addition, a large number of letters of intent were also signed. A similar result—though on a smaller scale—occurred in Tianjin, where close to 500 agreements worth 3.5 million yuan were signed in the span of just over one week. In order to popularize S&T achievements further, the central government under the SSTC has also created a National Market Development Center, which will aid in diffusing technology-related information to potential end-users. These domestic developments have also given impetus to a new and related thrust in Chinese policy, namely, expanded *exports* of technology from China.

The interesting feature of China's technology market is that the concept is being treated in a highly flexible manner. Relationships between research institutes and production enterprises can include joint development efforts, long-term cooperation agreements, joint bidding, foreign as well as domestic partners, and multiple players in any one of the previous ventures. Payments can be made based on royalties, a flat fee, or some combination of the two. In addition, a series of legal regulations are being devised to provide support structures to make the technology markets work. The leadership has even gone so far as to approve the creation of a venture capital company called China Venturetech

Investment Company.[19] The company will invest mainly in developing new technology for data processing, biotechnology, electronics and new materials.[20]

To accomplish its purpose of facilitating technology transfer, however, the technology market must depend on a rational price structure. Yet, price reform remains the Achilles' heel of the working of the technology market in China.[21] Chinese enterprise managers as well as research directors are frequently perplexed when it comes to the question of pricing, especially concerning the introduction of new products and components. Some of the more sophisticated attempts at price determination have tried to distinguish between (1) actual value—net income from the sale of a product using the technology; (2) secondary value—additional value of the product gained by applying the technology; and (3) latent value—the value of the potential number and/or types of applications for the technology. Yet, in spite of these efforts, pricing remains a serious problem and has already served to inhibit the effectiveness of this mechanism on a number of occasions.

A number of other factors have also plagued the technology market. First, many suppliers of technology, unable to determine an appropriate price for their technology, have been reluctant to offer their technology in the market for fear of creating a competitor. This continues to be the case in spite of the implementation of the national patent law in April 1985. Second, on a number of occasions, research units have offered unproven technologies, and, when expectations were not met, the purchaser held the developer directly responsible. Third, some units have intentionally engaged in fraud and deceit in order to make a profit, while others have plagiarized the research results of geographically distant research institutes and offered them for sale on the open market.[22]

The third element of the reforms deals with the absorption capabilities of enterprises.[23] In many respects, this problem is intimately associated with the issue of technical renovation—which involves a concerted effort by the State Economic Commission to modernize both plants and equipment within Chinese industry and to improve management techniques and related aspects in software production.[24] The goal of Chinese leaders is to transform the thinking of factory managers and to encourage them to think about technology as part of their competitive arsenal. Heretofore, most factory managers have been insensitive to the potential role of innovation in both the process and product dimensions of manufacturing. The current program to strengthen the buyers' capacity to utilize acquired technology is designed to provide the factory manager with a set of better tools for responding to the new economic environment in China—which was spelled out in the October 1984 Central Committee Decision on Reform of the Economic System.

Funds for technical transformation are to come from the central or local government in the form of both loans and grants. These funds, however, are only a means to help enterprises absorb some of the start-up costs for taking advantage of emerging market opportunities. In some respects, just as the changes in funding are desiged to encourage research institutes to seek out potential buyers of their technology, so the program of technical renovation is aimed at motivating enterprises to look for potential partners in the R&D community who can help them solve existing manufacturing problems, develop a new product, or improve the quality of an existing item.[25] Moreover, by changing the nature of enterprise behavior, the leadership hopes to create a demand-pull effect, thus improving the links between research and production.

The last element in the reform program concerns the treatment of S&T personnel. This problem has been the most difficult to resolve because of its broader political implications.[26] The reform document principally talks about the lack of mobility among S&T workers as a major defect in China's S&T modernization program. The problem affects students and scholars who have recently been sent abroad as well as individuals who have not left the PRC for overseas training.[27] According to Zhou Guangzhao, President of the CAS, this lack of mobility stifles creativity and inhibits the diffusion of technology and know-how within the society.[28] One major cause of the low mobility is the practice of inbreeding, whereby a university or research unit seeks to retain individuals it has trained. The aim of the reform is to provide a mechanism for talented S&T personnel to move to those places where their skills and expertise can be more fully and appropriately utilized.

The reforms regarding S&T personnel also aim to free up scientific and technical labor so that individuals with a certain type of expertise can serve as consultants or advisers to government offices, enterprises, etc. Once individuals complete their assigned duties, they are free to engage in off-duty consulting. Not only does such activity help supplement individual income, but it also facilitates the application of technical knowledge to problem-solving activities in the area of policy formulation and manufacturing.

Resistance to this element of the reform program has been widespread because political cadres see themselves as being displaced by scientific and technical personnel. Party officials have felt insecure in granting these individuals more authority and independence, especially since they threaten the Party's own claims to be the main purveyor of truth and knowledge in society. In addition, jealousy has emerged as some individuals can—and have—used their expertise to earn added income. In some cases, these individuals have been accused of extortion and blackmail by jealous individuals who have not had such opportunities.[29] There is also a concern that individuals will use existing resources and know-how to benefit themselves and ignore the larger needs of their unit or community. As a result of these continuing bottlenecks, the effort to alter the status and opportunities available to S&T personnel has encountered substantial problems. Finally, fears about personnel raiding have emerged. Institute directors, particularly those in remote areas, are concerned about losing their best talent to recruiters from the coastal areas who may try to entice key individuals to change jobs.

The reform document also touches on a number of other areas, some of them outside the immediate scope of this book. Two additional issues do deserve attention. First is the question of foreign technology imports. Generally speaking, the Chinese remain committed to the use of foreign technology and know-how. They have decided to de-emphasize the acquisition of whole plants and equipment and focus attention on the software side of technology imports. However, there is a growing debate. On one side are those who have immediate needs for equipment and therefore want to import such items as foreign-made computers and machinery; on the other side are those who seek to strengthen indigenous S&T capabilities and therefore are willing to forgo large numbers of final product purchases from abroad. In the area of microcomputers and television sets, for example, steps have already been taken to introduce protectionist methods to deter large-scale imports—suggesting that supporters of the latter position may have won the first round of this debate.

In the context of this analysis, the issue of foreign borrowing also holds some special importance because the current reform effort is modeled, in many ways, on that of the United States. The extent to which the idea of copying Western institutions is being criticized is reflected in an article in the January 1985 issue of *Keyan Guanli* (Science Research Management). In this article, the author—who is from the former Ministry of Machine-Building, sharply attacks the notion of "hiving off" research institutes to Chinese factories just because it is done that way in the West.[30] More specifically, the author suggests that while this may help stimulate new product development, it will necessarily lead these research institutes to ignore the economic plan as well as their larger social and national responsibilities.

More broadly, there has emerged growing concern that there has developed an excessive tendency to rely on foreign technology. In an important article in *Hongqi* (Red Flag), Zhang Aiping, Minister of Defense, raised the following issue:

> A tendency has emerged in the course of breaking away from national seclusion. In some comrades' opinion, it seems that everything foreign is good. They only think of reaping without sowing and of immediate interests regardless of national interests. They introduce foreign technology without serious consideration. As a result, foreign equipment which we can manufacture through our efforts after studying it is also imported, causing serious losses to the state and having a bad influence in the world.

More significantly, however, Zhang goes on to say:

> What merits particular attention is that some comrades turn a deaf ear to the repeated instructions of the CPC Central Committee. A similar situation can be found in our propaganda work. Comrades in charge of propaganda work have laid too much emphasis on imported equipment and production lines. They have not paid enough attention to the propagating of good products we have manufactured through our own efforts.[31]

Zhang's comments reflect China's continued commitment to achieving enhanced self-reliance in most technology areas. In effect, he is referring to previously mentioned problems of ineffective assimilation that continue to plague China.[32] A 1985 article in *Guangming Ribao* summed up China's desired approach: "Let us change as soon as possible the formula of 'the first machine being imported, the second machine being imported, and the third machine also being imported' into one of 'the first machine being imported, the second being made in China, and the third machine being exported.' "[33] These concerns about the proper approach to foreign technology acquisition and use suggest that there remain a number of unresolved policy issues regarding the real meaning of the open door.

The second issue deals with the effort to promote closer ties between the military and civilian sectors. Up until the early 1980s, the relationship between Chinese military and civilian R&D sectors had been highly compartmented. And, while CAS institutes and several key universities had frequently been tasked to participate in defense-related projects, the same could not be said for military R&D institutes with respect to most large civilian projects.[34] As noted in Chapter 1, the key to the successful performance of certain elements of the defense sector, e.g., strategic weapons programs, lies in the ability of a centralized agency at the top to attract a critical mass of individuals, create a team, and give it the necessary funds, equipment, and support to achieve its stated goal. Under the reforms, military units have been instructed to use their superior resources and more extensive experience in dealing with technology to help solve civilian problems.

In 1982, as part of a larger bureaucratic reform, the two primary offices for overseeing military R&D (National Defense Science and Technology Commission) and production (National Defense Industries Office) were combined into the National Defense Science, Technology and Industries Commission (NDSTIC). In some respects, this made the military R&D-production nexus a more powerful force in the bureaucracy—though at the time the effort to streamline military spending and close down obsolete production lines did offset some of this new acquired clout. More important, the NDSTIC retained much of its tasking authority. This decision, combined with the fact that defense S&T and production leaders see great potential benefit in helping to strengthen the civilian S&T base, suggests that the commitment to better civilian-military linkages will serve as a mechanism for broader defense involvement in all facets of the S&T modernization program—with the implication that in critical fields a strong central government role will continue to be present.

IMPLICATIONS FOR INNOVATION

So far, this chapter has presented a number of the key elements of China's S&T reform program, identifying the introduction of new market forces as well as continued reliance on centralized controls for bringing about closer links between research and production—and thus, it is hoped, more innovative behavior. Chinese leaders recognize that they cannot relinquish total control over S&T activities, especially since resources are limited and funding is in short supply. Concerns have already emerged that some research units are focusing on short-term goals and projects because of their immediate financial payoffs rather than concentrating on long-term issues and technological possibilities.[35] Thus, we are likely to see a continued effort to maintain an amalgam of authority and exchange structures to promote S&T modernization.

One of the most interesting results of this two-pronged strategy is the emergence of research-production alliances (*lianheti*). In some cases, these involve the coming together of research units, design units, and production enterprises into a single working entity. The gap between research and production is bridged as new product or design possibilities are addressed in a coordinated fashion. On several occasions, these alliances have involved organizations from different ministerial or administrative jurisdictions, suggesting that the *lianheti* may be a means to break down the bureaucratic barriers that heretofore have plagued China's S&T efforts.

The idea of the *lianheti* has been carried one step further by officials in China's Ministry of Machine-Building and Electronics Industry (MMBEI). According to a report in the *People's Daily*, electronics officials hope to establish ten large research-production complexes throughout China by the 1990s—though initially it seems that four areas will receive priority attention: Beijing, Shanghai, Guangdong, and Jiangsu provinces.[36] These complexes will include a number of research and production organizations from MMBEI as well as other ministries and localities. Their purpose is to facilitate links between research and production and to provide enhanced potential to respond to market opportunities for new components, final products, etc. Ideally, these complexes are to act more like American corporations than like administrative entities. They will compete with each other rather than specialize, although there will be some internal specialization. Whether or not they will behave as economic actors depends, to a great extent, on how far China's overall economic reforms proceed in the coming years and the extent to which authority structures give way to exchange mechanisms as the principal form of organization.

As China enters the post-Deng era, its strategy for S&T modernization and stimulating innovation will increasingly reflect the attempt to combine elements of state and market. State-led S&T policies—many of which will be a product of the leading group for S&T—will be aimed at developing an adequate infrastructure for promoting indigenous development and absorbing foreign technology, while the market will be used to ensure that enterprise and research managers are concerning themselves with innovation opportunities. This strategy is, in many respects, one that is converging more with many of the Asian newly industrialized nations than with the Soviet system that the Chinese emulated in the 1950s. In places such as India, Taiwan, and South Korea, a mixture of state and market is being used to establish a base for high technology industries such as very large-scale integration (VLSI) and computer development.

That China's reforms may be moving it more in the direction of other successful nations bodes well for the Chinese industrial innovation effort. China's leaders understand the nature of their country's problems and have already been modestly successful in offering a range of acceptable solutions to these problems. The role they have assigned to government is different from the stultifying role it played in the past. At the same time, however, there are strict limits to how far S&T reform can proceed in the future unless further political and economic reforms are introduced. In the political realm, these reforms will have to include a further diminished role for the Communist Party in the research sector as well as improvements in the status and treatment of S&T intellectuals. Some of this has begun with the recent house cleaning that has taken place at the level of China's municipal and provincial S&T commissions. In most large cities and provinces, new, technically competent individuals have been appointed to direct local S&T activities. In addition, many of these localities have also established their own leading groups for science and technology—a move that reinforces the continued role of government in S&T affairs. In Shanghai, for example, the local S&T leading group has been responsible for clarifying the S&T priorities of the municipality and mobilizing resources in such areas as microelectronics and biotechnology.

In the economic realm, further price reform is essential. Until there is substantial price reform, the technology market will not function effectively and the issue of price will limit the number of persons who will turn to this type of mechanism to sell or acquire technical know-how. Management training is another essential element. All too often, factory managers still consider technological innovation more of a bother than a benefit; they are afraid to accept the risk of employing a new product or component when they feel secure with existing technology. These managers need to understand better the role of technology in the firm and how to use technology to their advantage. Much work remains to be done.

The same types of problems exist within the research community. After "eating out of the big pot" for so long, many institutes are finding it difficult to escape from the ideology of the three dependences: dependence on the state for funding, on the upper level to designate research projects for the lower levels, and on others regarding the application of research results. In addition, apprehension about making mistakes is also widespread. Moreover, institute personnel, uncertain of the full meaning of the reforms or fearful of their consequences, have tried to emphasize the uniqueness of their research charters in an effort to block the reforms from taking hold at their institutions. It will take time to overcome these problems and build forward momentum for the reforms at the working level.

As indicated by former Premier Zhao Ziyang's comments at the Fourth Session of the Sixth NPC, the drive to reform and modernize science and technology has taken on added importance as Chinese leaders have sought to respond to what Toffler and others have claimed is the onset of a new global technological revolution. This new revolution is characterized by the significant role of four key technologies: microelectronics, computers, new materials, and biotechnology. China's leadership has decided to accept the challenge posed by this so-called technological revolution.

The notion of a global technological revolution is indeed attractive. In some instances, however, it has led the Chinese to forget history—that incremental progress in science and technology, not quantum leaps, has characterized the success stories in the development process. Even Japan, whose rapid growth has been held up as a potential model in China, made progress by improving existing technologies through modest innovations. While government did not play a huge role, it did play a significant role. The Japanese case shows that it is not the quantity, but rather the quality and nature of government intervention that counts.

Most important, the effort to attain substantial levels of growth and technological advance can only be accomplished after a workable S&T infrastructure has been put in place. Policies for science and technology are part of an entire package, involving all sorts of inputs ranging from finance to marketing. Over the last year, China has taken some bold steps to reaffirm the importance of S&T and to stimulate forward momentum. The success of this effort will not come from adhering in a rigid fashion to catchy themes or by pursuing strategies that are based on the political fear of falling behind. Rather, the long-term viability of China's present mixed strategy will be in allowing the strategy to evolve in conjunction with the further changes that are needed in the economic system. Government policy can only have its desired impact when the economic signals being sent to the various actors in the system are, on balance, logical and internally consistent. In this regard, Deng Xiaoping appears correct; what is needed is a Chinese type of modernization. China may develop a model for combining state-led initiatives with market forces in a more effective way than either most developing nations or most socialist countries have been able to achieve. The case of Shanghai's efforts to advance its electronics capabilities and stimulate greater innovation reflects the playing out of many of the forces described above.

NOTES

1. Jan Prybyla, *Market and Plan Under Socialism: The Bird in the Cage* (Stanford, Calif.: Hoover Institution Press, 1987).
2. Charles E. Lindblom, *Politics and Markets* (New York: Basic Books, 1977).
3. Denis Fred Simon, "Rethinking R&D," *China Business Review,* July–August 1983, pp. 25–31.
4. Nancy Dorfman, "Route 128: The Development of a Regional High Technology Economy," *Research Policy* (December 1983): 299–316.
5. Song Jian quoting Deng Xiaoping in "Science Reforms Vital," *Science,* August 9, 1985, p. 526.
6. R.P. Suttmeier, *Science, Technology and China's Drive for Modernization* (Stanford: Hoover Institution Press, 1980). Leo Orleans, ed., *Science in Contemporary China* (Stanford: Stanford University Press, 1981).
7. *Foreign Broadcast Information Service—People's Republic of China,* March 28, 1986, p. K11.
8. *Beijing Review,* November 15, 1982, pp. 13–20.
9. *Foreign Broadcast Information Service—People's Republic of China* January 31, 1983, p. K8.
10. During interviews in Beijing in March 1988, it was suggested that the S&T leading group might be abolished. The main reason was because it ostensibly achieved its goal of reinforcing the high-level importance of S&T, and therefore the rationale for its existence had disappeared. What follows in no way conflicts with this reasoning. It merely indicates that the message sent by former Premier Zhao Ziyang has been delivered and generally has been well received.
11. See Denis Fred Simon and Detlef Rehn, "Innovation in China's Semiconductor Industry: The Case of Shanghai," *Research Policy* 16, no. 5 (October 1987): 259–277.
12. Ma Lili, "The Concept of China's Scientific Research Reform: A Visit to Wu Mingyu, Vice-Minister of the State Science and Technology Commission," *Huashengbao,* April 10, 1985, p. 31, translated in *Joint Publications Research Service—China Science and Technology 85–028,* August 27, 1985, p. 1.

13. Dai Yaping, "Running Water Flows Into the Scientific and Technological Circles in China," *Zhongguo Xinwen She,* March 20, 1985, translated in *Foreign Broadcast Information Service—People's Republic of China,* March 26, 1985, p. K10.

14. "CPC Central Committee's 13 March 1985 Decision on the Reform of the Science and Technology Management System," *Xinhua,* March 19, 1985, translated in *Foreign Broadcast Information Service—People's Republic of China,* March 21, 1985, pp. K1–9.

15. According to Chinese estimates up to 1985, China spends about 0.6 percent of its national income on R&D, while the industrialized countries spend between 2 and 3 percent. More recent data indicates, however, that actual R&D spending in China may be in the range of 1.2 to 1.4 percent of GNP.

16. *Foreign Broadcast Information Service—People's Republic of China,* March 21, 1985, pp. K2–3.

17. *China Daily,* January 8, 1985, p. 1.

18. "The Technical Market Must Serve Economic Construction: An Interview with Guo Shuyuan, Vice Minister of the State Science and Technology Commission," *Liaowang,* May 27, 1985, pp. 38–39, translated in *Joint Publications Research Service—China Science and Technology 85–038,* November 5, 1985, p. 3.

19. "New Ideas to Get Funds Despite Risk," *China Daily,* January 13, 1986, p. 3.

20. Ironically, 40 percent of the capital for the 40 million yuan company has come from the State Science and Technology Commission, raising questions about how market driven decisions on investments might ultimately be.

21. Xu Yi, Chen Baosen, and Liang Wuxia, *Shehuizhuyi Jiage Wenti* (Beijing: Chinese Finance and Economics Press, 1982) translated in *Joint Publications Research Service—China Economic Affairs 85–019,* February 20, 1985, esp. pp. 75–80.

22. Richard P. Suttmeier, "New Conflicts in the Research Environment," *Bulletin of the Atomic Scientists,* October 1984, pp. 7S–11S.

23. See Li Boxi et al., *Zhongguo Jishu Gaizao Wenti Yanjiu* (Analysis of the Problems Regarding China's Technical Transformation), vols. 1–2 (Shanxi: People's Publishing House, 1984).

24. "Technical Renovation Is the Catchword," *Intertrade,* October 1985, pp. 9–13.

25. *Hongqi* (Red Flag), August 16, 1985, pp. 28–33, translated in *Joint Publications Research Service—China Red Flag 85–021,* October 15, 1985, p. 57.

26. See Denis Fred Simon, "China's S&T Intellectuals in the Post-Mao Era: A Retrospective and Prospective Glimpse," *Journal of Northeast Asian Studies,* Summer 1985, pp. 57–82.

27. "Returned Students Feeling Stifled," *China Daily,* August 31, 1984, p. 4.
28. *Guangming Ribao,* December 21, 1984, p. 1, translated in *Joint Publications Research—China Science and Technology 85–010,* June 12, 1985, pp. 22–24.
29. "Guanxi Reports on Persecution of Engineer," translated in *Foreign Broadcast Information Service—People's Republic of China,* July 20, 1984, p. P3.
30. Zhang Xicheng, "Jixie Gongye Keyan Tizhi Gaige Zongshu" (An Outline of the Reforms in the Scientific Research System of the Machine-Building Industry), *Keyan Guanli* (Scientific Research Management), January 1985, pp. 26–28.
31. Zhang Aiping, "Strengthen Leadership and Do a Better Job in Importing Technology," *Hongqi,* no. 24, December 16, 1985, pp. 4–9.
32. "Strive for Self-Development," *Tianjin Ribao,* October 18, 1985, p. 1.
33. *Guangming Ribao,* July 4, 1985, p. 1.
34. One piece of evidence that this has begun to change is the active involvement of many of the scientists formerly involved in China's nuclear weapons program in the country's nuclear energy program.
35. Two party cadres from the Yantai S&T Commission in Shandong recently received disciplinary warnings for using scientific research funds and equipment to make business deals. They used Scientific Equipment Company affiliated with the commission to sell equipment under the guise of scientific exchange. *China Daily,* September 19, 1985.
36. *Renmin Ribao* (People's Daily), July 17, 1986, p. 1; Zhang Feng, "Li Tieying yi du tan" (Discussion with Li Tieying), *Shijie Jingji Daobao,* no. 300, August 4, 1986, p. 15.

3 STRATEGIC GUIDELINES FOR CHINA'S ELECTRONICS INDUSTRY

The development of a modern electronics industry will bring about a big leap forward for our industry, and it will be a starting point for a new industrial revolution in the history of China. The rapid popularisation of modern electronic technology will make China the first newly industrialized socialist power with first-rate electronic technology.

—Liu Shaoqui

Since the early 1970s, the global economy has been undergoing a basic restructuring. The "oil crisis" of 1973 engendered the end of a pattern of industrialization which had characterized the process of economic development since the 19th century. At the same time, it also paved the way for the onset of the "electronics and information revolution," a revolution that is characterized by the expanded emphasis on the production, storage, and distribution of information as a central economic and technological activity.[1] By taking advantage of the numerous advances and cost reductions in microelectronics e.g. large-scale integrated circuits, the Chinese leadership has created a new basis for economic and social development.[2] The full importance of these changes has only now been fully recognized by developed and developing nations alike—stimulated, in large part, by the potential economic and technological benefits emerging from the convergence of electronics, telecommunications and computerization.

The "electronics and information revolution" is characterized by a number of basic features. In contrast to the second industrial revolution that took place in Europe in the late nineteenth and early twentieth centuries—a revolution based on the assumption of an abundance of energy, raw materials, and natural resources—the electronic revolution of the late twentieth century is both energy and materials-saving.[3] Moreover, while in retrospect the industrial revolution rested mainly on such conventional economic inputs as capital and labor, the electronics and information revolution is characterised by its intensive reliance on knowledge and high skill levels as the underpinning of overall progress.[4] Thirdly, the electronics and information revolution is universal in character. Especially with respect to microelectronics, it has steadily, albeit gradually in some cases, permeated all sectors of the economy and society.[5]

A fourth feature of the electronics and information revolution is its global character.[6] In view of the rapidly increasing financial requirements to carry out research and development and innovation, new technologies are of necessity more and more developed in an international framework. The internationalization of R&D (and production) in electronics and computer industry has led to the gradual emergence of new patterns of regional concentration in overall industry structure. While the industrial revolution resulted in the establishment of only a limited number of mostly heavy industry-oriented economic centers, notably in Western Europe and the United States, the global character of the electronics and information revolution has made it possible for high-technology centers to emerge throughout various parts of the world. This fact helps to explain why today the Asia-Pacific Rim (notably Japan, South Korea, and Taiwan) has emerged as one of the most dynamic areas of the global electronics and computer industry.[7]

All of these changes have not gone unnoticed in China. As suggested above, the Chinese have undertaken major steps to create an infrastructure for electronics research and production, not only to close the prevailing technological gap between China and the industrialized nations, but also, eventually, to allow the country to share global technological leadership in electronics with the industrialized nations. Throughout the process, the Chinese leadership has been confronted with a fundamental dilemma: with the possible exception of its "young" software sector, the development pattern of China's electronics and computer industry over the last thirty years has resulted in the emergence of structures which constrain China from following the example of other developing countries, e.g. South Korea and Taiwan. The same structural factors also inhibit China from leapfrogging several stages of technological development and thus shortening the process of catching up. Indeed, many of the factors mentioned above with respect to the overall S&T system also affect the electronics industry, such as the relationships and contradictions between plan and market, centralization and decentralization, the military and the civilian sector, R&D and production, and prototype and new product development.

This chapter gives an overview of some of the historical conditions under which China has established its electronics industry. It analyzes development strategies for the electronic sector, highlighting the different approaches and perceptions of the Chinese leadership towards electronics. The discussion also identifies the major obstacles to further development of the electronics industry and illustrates the changes in the role and status of the electronics sector in China's overall economic and social development.

HISTORICAL DIMENSIONS OF THE ELECTRONICS INDUSTRY: 1956 TO 1978

The beginnings of a systematic approach to the development of an indigenous Chinese electronics industry go back to the mid-1950s. Within the twelve-year plan promulgated for science and technology in 1956, electronics was accorded a priority role.[8] This plan, elaborated with the support of Soviet scientists, defined a number of key projects whose completion, it was thought, would create a solid scientific and technological foundation. With respect to electronics in particular, the plan stressed the areas of computer technology, semiconductors, automation technology, and general electronics technology. Through the concentration of critical manpower and material and financial resources on a few projects, several achievements of national importance were soon realized. As early as 1958, China developed its first computer, only one year after Japan had done the same. China's first transistor was developed in 1960; its technological level represented a gap of about four years vis-à-vis the Soviet Union, which at that time was still actively supporting the Chinese efforts.[9]

Generally speaking, the development history of China's electronics industry prior to 1978 can be seen in terms of two seemingly contradictory characterics. On the one hand, the high concentration of overall investment has contributed to the creation of a substantial set of R&D and production capabilities. For the most part, these capabilities were oriented toward and/or responsive to the demands of the defense sector; the establishment of a dynamic civilian-oriented electronics industry was not a major objective. On the other hand, in spite of the appreciable achievements of the electronics sector during its early history, there also emerged a number of basic problems, especially in the area of technological innovation, which still remain an object of concern today.

The most salient aspects of the electronics industry in China are its structural similarities with the economic and technological structure of the overall Soviet system. Like many other Chinese industries, the electronics industry was characterized by the verticalization of its organizational structure and the high barriers between R&D and production, including limited interaction between researchers and end-users. Even today, China's computer industry is distinguished by the separation of developers, manufacturers, and users. New approaches to develop the computer industry in a more integrated manner, i.e. the coordinated and interrelated development of hard and software, peripherals, service and maintenance, personnel training, etc., although theoretically being implemented, are still far from being realized.

A second feature of the electronics industry has been its primary military orientation. As stated previously, China's electronics sector developed in response to the requirements of the Chinese military, and therefore was nurtured and protected by the military in a number of ways.[10] For example, considerations of cost and efficiency were frequently subordinated to meeting defense requirements and standards. A significant portion of production was highly specialized, customized, and small-scale in terms of production quantities. Moreover, the electronics industry, as with several of the other "ministries of machine building," was part of a highly compartmented bureaucratic apparatus, with few incentives or mechanisms for cross-fertilization and interaction.

In effect, the concentration of resources on military electronics led to the appearance of a number of biases in research and production activities.[11] For example, the development of China's computer industry over many years was focused on stand-alone machines for scientific calculations and the processing of large quantities of numbers. The result of this emphasis was that operational speed and memory size were regarded as the most important computer parameters, while software and peripheral development lagged very far behind. Equally important was the fact that the appropriate incentives for serial computer production did not emerge on their own. Out of over two hundred different models of small, medium, and large computers, only ten were produced in quantities greater than fifty units.[12]

The military orientation of the industry also resulted in very limited access to foreign technology. Aside from capital investment by the central government, the modernization of the research and production facilities through external stimuli or the regular upgrading of the equipment in use through foreign imports was very difficult, particularly after the Soviet pullout in 1960. Finally, the widespread absence of a set of civilian and consumer-oriented electronics research and production facilities and the lack of horizontal technology transfers from the military into the civilian sectors restricted the modernization of this Chinese industry and effectively precluded it from becoming a major industrial sector in China's economic development prior to 1978.

Military orientation of the electronics industry found its foremost expression in the political squabbles which predominated in the 1960s and early 1970s. Eventually, the development of the electronics sector suffered because it had become enmeshed in the political disputes and struggles within the central leadership. The best example of the politicization of the industry is reflected in the "steel versus electronics" debate which took place in 1971 and 1972.[13] A "steel faction" in the Chinese leadership believed that an emphasis on steel and other similar industries would be the best way to close the prevailing urban and rural gap. They considered steel a core industry for overall economic development, without which China could not develop its own means of production. The "electronics faction" stressed the role of modern technologies, in particular electronics, as the driving force for development. Electronics symbolized a development strategy that was more urban-based and dependent on large-scale production systems similar to those established abroad.[14]

Along with the obvious political salience of the debate, it has had relevance in several other key areas. Most important, it touched on a number of basic problems regarding China's overall development policy: military versus civilian needs, self-reliance versus acquisition of foreign know-how and equipment, basic research versus applied and industry-oriented research, and centralized versus decentralized development strategy. Unfortunately for China, electronics therefore became the whipping boy for a number of contending political groups anxious to push ahead in favor of the position of the steel faction for reasons often unrelated to the merits of China's electronics strategy or development capabilities.

However, within the broad framework of political debates, the electronics sector was, for the first time, discussed not only as one industrial sector among others, but in its function as the potential core sector which could have a critical impact on all other areas of the economy and society. It was somewhat remarkable that the debate developed as it did and that electronics was highlighted as a potentially core technology area, especially since the global electronics and informatics revolution was only beginning to take off in the industrialized West and Japan. Although in 1971 and 1972 the time was not ripe, technologically or politically, for supporting an "electronics first" position in China, the debate nevertheless prepared the ground for the redefinition of the role of the electronics industry in the late 1970s.

THE STRUCTURE AND ORGANIZATION OF CHINA'S ELECTRONICS INDUSTRY

China's electronics industry can be broken down into six major product areas: (1) television, radio, and recording equipment; (2) computers; (3) radar and communication equipment; (4) electronic components; (5) professional and industrial electronics instrumentation and equipment; and (6) military electronics. The industry has multiple ministerial-level organizations with an interest in the research, production, and application aspects of electronics technology, components, or equipment. Also of critical importance are a series of similar research and production units under the control of provincial and municipal authorities. At times, the mere presence of these numerous organizations has created intense rivalry and competition as each of the respective ministries and localities has desired to have its own infrastructure for meeting its electronics needs. Table 3–1 presents a list of the key ministries engaged in electronics.

While there are several key ministries involved in China's electronics industry, the primary one has been the Ministry of Electronics Industry (MEI), formerly called the Fourth Ministry of Machine-Building. (See Figure 3–1.) Prior to a number of changes introduced in 1986, the MEI administered the majority of the 2600 factories in the country's electronics industry along with over 130 research institutes and 6 dedicated universities focused on electronics technology. (There were 172 enterprises under its formal jurisdiction.) Presently, the extent of MEI control varies as a result of the divestment decision in late 1985, whereby MEI

Table 3-1.   Key Ministries in China's Electronics Industry.

Name	Primary Interest		
	R&D	*Production*	*Application*
Ministry of Electronics Industry*	x	x	x
Ministry of Space Industry	x	x	x
Ministry of Aeronautics Industry	x	x	x
State Machine-Building Commission	x	x	x
Ministry of Posts and Tele-communication	x	x	x
Ministry of Railways			x
Ministry of Public Security			x
People's Bank			x
Ministry of Metallurgy	x		
Ministry of Transport			x
Ministry of Water Resources	x		x
Ministry of Light Industry			x

Source: *Zhongguo Dianzi Gongye Nianjian* (Chinese Electronics Yearbook) Beijing, 1986).

*Note: The Ministry of Electronics Industry and the State Machine-Building Commission were merged in April 1988.

relinquished control over the day-to-day management of its enterprises *and* the degree to which local authorities are involved in overseeing the operation of specific units.[15]

In early 1987, a major structural reform was implemented within the MEI. MEI was selected (along with the former Ministry of Machine-Building) to be one of the first to undergo reorganization in conjunction with the leadership's decision to separate political management from economic administration at both the enterprise and policy-making levels. The success achieved in carrying out this reform may have had a lot to do with the decision to appoint MEI Minister Li Tieying (who became MEI Minister in the summer of 1985) to head the State Commission for Economic Restructuring under the State Council later in the year.

Heretofore, the MEI has been divided into five main bureaus: communication, broadcasting and television; microelectronics; systems engineering (radar and navigation); electronic devices and components; and computer and information industries. The computer bureau was the former State Administration of Computer Industry (SACI), which was incorporated into the MEI structure during the May 1982

Figure 3–1.   China's Electronics Industry.

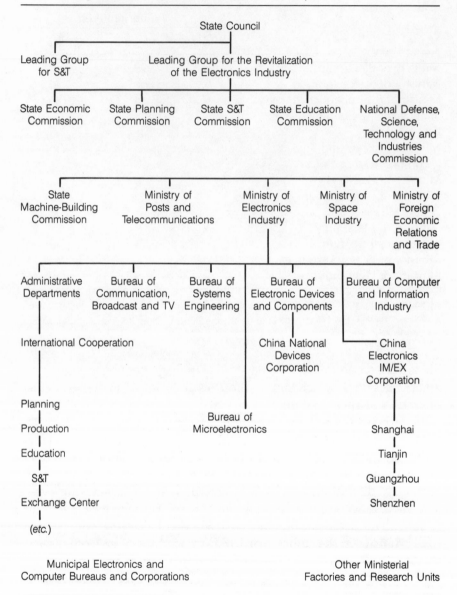

Source: Ministry of Electronics Industry (Beijing, July 1987).

Note: In April 1988, two major changes took place. The State Machine-Building Commission and the Ministry of Electronics Industry were merged into the Ministry of Machine-Building and Electronics Industry. In addition, the State Economic Commission and the State Planning Commission were combined into a new organization called the State Planning Commission.

bureaucratic reform. In contrast to the previous departmental structure, each of the bureaus will be playing more of a macro-oriented policymaking role rather than one of directly administering the affairs of its subordinate units at the micro level.

More specifically, each functional bureau under the MEI oversees a series of manufacturing and research facilities. For example, under the bureau responsible for computers and informatics, there is a fully articulated R&D and industrial structure containing 130 enterprises and 26 research units. In some cases, however, this oversight role has been superseded by other, simultaneous forms of structural reorganization. A good case in point involves the creation of four major computer conglomerates (*jituan gongsi*) in the cities of Beijing (*Changcheng*), Shanghai (*Changjiang*), Shenyang (*Changbai*), and Guangzhou (*Changling*). The Changcheng Computer Conglomerate, which is also known as the Great Wall Computer Corporation, is composed of fifty-eight existing computer production units, four R&D institutes and five universities—all of which have been drawn from MEI, the CAS, and the Beijing Municipal government.[16] The group is responsible for all phases of research, manufacturing, sales and service, and training. It operates as an integrated entity, fostering horizontal coordination and minimizing administrative interference from the local or central government. The core of the group is the China Computer Development Corporation, which is composed of six smaller computer companies. A similar type of "conglomerization" has taken place in Shanghai with the formation of the Yangtze River Computer Group Conglomerate.

Outside of these new conglomerates, there are a host of other management and control amalgams. According to Chinese statements, after the divestment only two key enterprises remain under the direct control of MEI.[17] It appears, however, that the divestment did not necessarily include those factories that are purely military-oriented; while the MEI may continue to provide these factories with operational funds, most of their project money appears to come from the NDSTIC or other military-related organizations. In other cases, while the divestment decision provided for the devolution of administrative responsibility from the central to the local governments, it appears that the principle of dual leadership (*shuangzhong lingdao*) is still being followed. That is, enterprises are jointly administered by a combination of central and local authorities.[18] In Beijing municipality, a special office was created to manage the affairs of the divested enterprises; its principal purpose was to ensure that the factories received adequate infrastructural support, i.e. electricity and water, as well as raw materials and related inputs. Even today, as officials try to clarify the lines of managerial oversight and responsibility, one Chinese official said that there can be as many as ten different organizational forms involving different mixtures of administrative control.[19]

Similar types of organizational arrangements exist under the other ministries mentioned above, such as the MSI, which has a number of branch factories and research institutes located in cities such as Shanghai. Many of these ministries, however, have yet to undergo the extensive restructuring that has taken place in the MEI. Understanding these organizational principles—past, present and future—goes a long way toward clarifying why decision making in China can be so complex and why it is so difficult to carry out successful innovation efforts. The Chinese refer to these complexities in organizational structure as the *tiao tiao kuai kuai* problem, whereby horizontal coordination is hard to implement because of the extreme vertical nature of the bureaucratic apparatus.

Because of this highly complex and differentiated organizational setting, the electronics industry, like many other Chinese industries, has been plagued with the general problems of overlapping jurisdictions and lack of clear-cut lines of decision making. It is often difficult for Chinese as well as foreigners to know who has authority or responsibility for making various decisions about setting priorities, sourcing and pricing inputs, managing particular projects, or initiating relationships between R&D units and potential end-users.

Of the major changes in policy and organization which have been introduced to overcome these difficulties since the early 1980s, the most prominent has been the creation of the State Council Leading Group for the Revitalization of the Electronics Industry (*Guowuyuan Dianzi Zhenxing Lingdao Xiao Zu*). It has been headed by Premier Li Peng and is designed to ameliorate the coordination problems that have dominated China's efforts to develop its electronics industry. Sitting on the leading group are high-level representatives from the leading government commissions and key ministries. (See Figure 3–2.) The group is actually divided into three tiers. The composition of the first tier includes Premier Li Peng plus five persons at the minister and vice-minister level representing the State Economic Commission (SEC), the State S&T Commission (SSTC), the Ministry of Labor and Personnel (MLP), the National Defense Science, Technology, and Industry Commission (NDSTIC) and the Ministry of Electronics Industry (MEI). A second tier composed of approximately fifteen members includes representatives from those organizations associated with the research,

Figure 3–2. Leading Group for the Revitalization of the Electronics Industry.

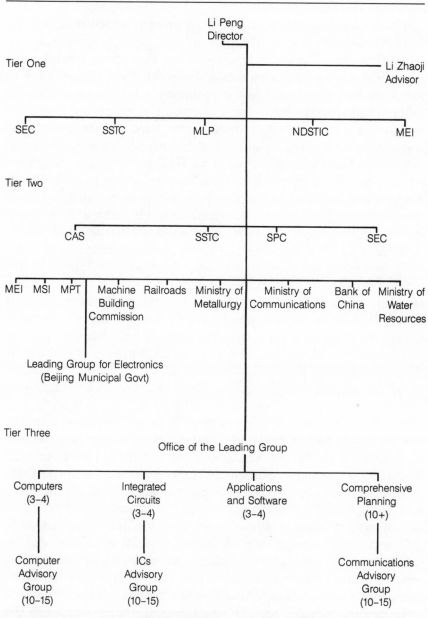

Note: Advisory Group Members are from key universities and research institutes throughout the country. Numbers in parentheses refer to the number of persons in the section or group.

production, and/or application side of the electronics and computer industry. For example, the CAS and the State Planning Commission (SPC) are represented.

The third tier, which has the greatest substantive responsibility for China's overall electronics and computer development strategy, is represented by the office of the leading group. This office, headed by Li Xianglin, a former official in the MEI and the SPC, is actually where policy inputs are made and policy recommendations are provided. The office is staffed by about twenty permanent members and is divided into four main functional subgroups: integrated circuits; computers; applications and software; and comprehensive affairs, including communications and telecommunications. Under each of the subgroups (except for applications and software) sits an advisory group, which is composed of ten to fifteen persons drawn from major research institutes, universities, and related organizations from around the country. These advisory groups provide expert advice to the office, which then reports to the ministerial and commission representatives.

Aside from its broad policymaking powers across a number of important ministries, there are several important aspects to this leading group. First, the budget and salary of the office have been provided directly by the State Council, which gives this body greater independence than in the past, when the various members of the office were paid by their respective ministries. Second, also represented on the national-level leading group have been representatives from the Beijing leading group for electronics industry, which is an office under the Beijing Municipality. In spite of the advanced technological capabilities of places such as Shanghai, Beijing has been the only geographic entity formally represented on this leading group. This perhaps reflects the large number of factories and research institutes situated in Beijing that are operated by the central government, such as the research institutes under the CAS.

Third, the mandate of the leading group was expanded in January 1985 to include communications, a field that heretofore had been outside of its jurisdiction.[20] It is also concentrating its attention on component production, such as the development of large-scale integration (LSI), to support indigenous production of consumer products, computers, etc. This means that all sectors which are of strategic importance to the future development of China's electronics industry will be supervised by the leading group. This is, however, not in contrast to the strides for decentralization. With respect to the "mass production of quality, inexpensive and multifunctional products," market competition will be allowed to "eliminate inferior and overpriced products from the market."[21]

Fourth, while the leading group does not have a specific budget for project allocation, through its policy formulation function it works directly through the State Planning Commission and other high level government bodies to ensure that ample funds are made available for priority projects and technology imports. In some cases, these funds are made available through a newly established process of tenders and bids that provide a mechanism for various research and/or production units to compete for monies for national projects.

It also should be noted that the State Economic Commission (now incorporated into the State Planning Commission) plays an important role in the electronics industry through the funds it provides for "technical transformation" and plant renovation. For example, in the Sixth Five Year Plan, the SEC selected 550 key projects in the machinery and electronics industries to receive special funds for plant modernization and acquisition of key equipment; 148 of these projects were focused, directly and indirectly, on the electronics industry.[22] In addition, out of the 3000 key technology import projects identified in the Sixth FYP, approximately 60 were in the electronics industry. According to MEI officials, an expanded sum of funds will be allocated for both these purposes in the Seventh Five Year Plan (1986 to 1990).

ELECTRONICS AND THE FOUR MODERNIZATIONS DRIVE

The inception of the four modernizations program in 1978 led to a new attitude towards the role of electronics in China's economic development. Designating science and technology as cornerstones for China's future development, the post-Mao leadership identified electronics as the "hallmark of a country's level of modernization." At the National Science Conference of March 1978, electronics, especially semiconductor and computer technology, was declared a key priority area. The National Development Plan for Science and Technology (1978–85) set very ambitious goals for electronics. For example, the attainment within seven years of the capabilities for LSI mass production, the creation of a base for very large-scale integration (VLSI) research, the building of supercomputers, the establishment of large computer networks, and the widespread application of computers within China's key enterprises to control and manage the production process better.[23] Moreover, in view of China's very limited technological and manufacturing potential, it was made clear that a massive influx of foreign technology was needed to parallel domestic efforts to attain the stated targets for the electronics industry.

The ambitious nature of the objectives reflected the peculiarity of the Chinese situation at that time. The open-door policy and the liberation of scientists, economists, and planners from Maoist ideological constraints led to a new atmosphere in which everything and anything seemed possible. Although disillusionment was soon felt when the targets of the modernization program had to be adjusted, the strategic outline of the 1978 S&T plan remained important for two main reasons.

First, the definition of electronics as the hallmark of modernization—which is remarkably similar to the formulation used in the steel versus electronics debate—reflected the growing awareness of Chinese planners that electronics technology is not confined to national defense applications, but has an overall relevance for all sectors of the economy and society.[24] Second, although in the 1960s and 1970s the development orientation of China's electronics industry leaders was somewhat akin to emerging international patterns, they lacked a clear appreciation of the strength and weaknesses of the country's own electronics sector. The approach they adopted did not reflect a coherent strategy for closing the gap with the industrialized countries in R&D and production.

In 1978, although the leadership mostly continued to overestimate the technical capabilities of their system, a set of relatively more coherent proposals were put forth, directed towards improvements in a few select areas regarded as critical for the future development of the whole electronics sector, which also promised to close the gap in a fairly short time. Moreover, the leadership exhibited greater sensitivity to developments taking place abroad in electronics. In essence, it acknowledged that the previous strategy of self-reliance needed to be reconsidered and re-evaluated. These changes provided the basis for a new relationship between technology and politics in Chinese development strategy.

After confronting a plethora of personnel, production, and resource bottlenecks that thwarted attempts to catapult the electronics industry, the Chinese became aware that the original targets for electronics development were overambitious. This awareness led to the search for a new strategy for electronics modernization, beginning in 1982. This search was characterized by several factors.

First, the new strategic goal of the Chinese modernization policy promulgated at the Twelfth Congress of the Chinese Communist Party in

1982—the quadrupling of the 1980 agricultural and industrial gross production value by the year 2000—resulted in the public discovery of the productive character of electronics technology. Broad application of electronics in each economic sector promised improvements in labor productivity and product quality and therefore offered the potential for a substantial increase in revenues to the government, central and local. This recognition provided the impetus for giving expanded attention to the civilian side of the electronics industry. Consequently, within the Chinese leadership the focus of attention shifted to include *application* as a priority goal of electronics modernization. This new strategic orientation led the computer industry to place new emphasis on the manufacture of user-friendly mini- and microcomputers, on peripheral equipment, and especially on software to support broad computerization—all of which were geared to civilian needs.

Second, as in other economic sectors, the Chinese leadership recognized the need for basic structural reforms of the electronics industry in order to realize their short-term and long-term goals. Within this context, a number of obstacles were identified as major barriers to the development of electronics. These included:

1. The organizational structure. It was strongly vertical in nature, both functionally (between research and production) and geographically (between central and local institutions); this explains the generally low level of innovation in the electronics sector.
2. The pattern of regional dispersion of the electronics industry, which does not correspond to the requirements of specialization, the division of labor, and economic efficiency.
3. The low technological level of existing enterprises, exemplified by the generally backward state of manufacturing technologies. This helps to explain the low level of competitiveness of electronic products originating from China.
4. The low skill levels of workers and staff, the inefficient use of the qualified personnel, and the absence of institutionalized procedures for regular skills upgrading and enhancement.

For China, 1983 marked an important transition point in the development of the electronics industry. One crucial element was the growing attention given to the relevance for China of the so-called new technological revolution in the West; for the first time the development strategy of China's electronics sector was discussed from the perspective of the global economic and technological environment. For instance, faced with a lagging export capability, the Chinese started to consider international standards and quality criteria as necessary requirements for entering the world market. Most important, the Chinese also began to identify electronics as a pioneer industry. The electronics industry came to be regarded as a vital sector responsible for leading the development of all other industrial and economic sectors; this was one aspect of the pervasive impact of the microelectronics revolution. (See Table 3-2.)

Another aspect of the transition was a series of discussions in the Chinese press on economic and S&T issues that presaged important policy changes at the central level. The electronics industry was selected as an area of experimentation for a number of the economic and S&T reforms, most notably technical transformation of the existing research and production facilities. Production capacity for a range of consumer and industrial electronics products was also expanded through a combination of increased capital construction and technical renovation. All of these measures were, in one way or another, designed to stimulate improved productivity and technological advance in an industry that was increasingly viewed as a vital link in the four modernizations program—though differences of opinion did appear over the pace of advance and the need for making quantum leaps forward.

Chinese policy goals and intentions for electronics were most clearly reflected in January 1985 in a document entitled "The Strategy for the Development of China's Electronics and Information Industries."[25] This document is significant for a number of reasons, one being that it was issued in the immediate aftermath of the Central Committee Decision on the Reform of the Economic System, which laid out a program for allowing market forces to play a more distinct role in stimulating

Table 3-2. Electronics as a Percentage of Industrial Output (in billion yuan; prices of 1980).

Year	1981	1982	1983	1984	1985	1986	1987
GVIO (a)	517.8	557.7	614.7	702.9	829.8	1157.0	1378.0
Electronics (b)	11.9	11.8	14.0	23.4	28.6	30.6	40.8
(b) as percentage of (a)	2.3	2.1	2.3	3.3	3.5	2.7	3.0

Source: State Statistical Bureau, *Statistical Yearbook of China*, 1981–1986 (Beijing, 1987). Also, Ministry of Electronics Industry, Beijing, 1988).

economic development. Essentially, the document sets the framework for the development of China's electronics industry during the Seventh Five Year Plan (1986 to 1990) and beyond. It was formulated and issued by the aforementioned State Council Leading Group for the Revitalization of the Electronics Industry, formerly known as the State Council Leading Group for the Computer and LSI Industry and originally established in late 1982. The pronouncement of the new strategy for electronics was the first formal effort by this governmental body to coordinate and direct the various activities in the electronics field.

The strategic guidelines elaborated for the electronics industry can be summarized, as follows:

1. The overall goal of the industry is expanded application of electronics technology in order to serve better the development of the national economy and society. The popularization of microcomputers, for example, is to be stressed along with software, especially Chinese character programs.

2. The acquisition and assimilation of foreign technology are to be stressed as a means to closing the prevailing gap between China and the rest of the world. Joint ventures and other forms of cooperation are to be encouraged. These measures aim to complement indigenous R&D and manufacturing programs in order to "speed up the development of China's electronics industry in order to attain advanced world levels sooner and thereby increase our capacity for self-reliance."

3. Greater attention should be paid to creating a fully articulated and integrated electronics industry, capable of supplying needed components and manufacturing equipment as well as final products. Within this context, the main goal is "to achieve economical, large-scale mass production with good quality and low cost." Special attention will be given to large-scale integrated circuits; the short-term goal will be "to master selected, suitable, and advanced LSI circuits."

4. Efforts should be made to establish an effective balance between centralization and decentralization in the management of the electronics industry. Market regulation, competition, and joint production will be used to transform or eliminate inferior, expensive products. Electronics products that require large investment, long production time, and high technology, e.g. LSI, must be produced under unified state planning and unified arrangements in order to avoid blind development and waste of time, manpower and materials.

5. There should be close coordination and integration in the development of the electronics, computers and telecommunications industries.
6. The state should adopt a series of policies designed to move away from a system of top-down grants and establish a new system based on competitive bids. While the state should continue to invest money in key projects that are of decisive national importance, it is not enough to rely on the state alone. Foreign investment should also be more effectively utilized as a source of capital to build up the electronics industry.

In line with the managerial role of the leading group as a coordinating administrative body, these guidelines provide a framework for directing investment, training, and R&D activities. Similarly, in a major speech at a conference of leading cadres of the electronics industry which was held in January 1986 in Beijing the new minister of the MEI, Li Tieying, presented the objectives for electronics during the Seventh Five Year Plan.[26] (See Table 3–3.) Except for a few exceptions, the layout of the Seventh FYP for the electronics industry is consistent with the themes present in early 1985.

The importance of the 1986 guidelines and development targets lies in a number of areas. First, they represent a further refinement of existing strategy as well as providing a comprehensive set of goals and measures designed to assist development of an industry which has been slated to play a decisive role in the country's overall modernization. By presenting a detailed set of the guidelines, the State Council leading group hoped to gain better control over the rate and locus of activity than in the past, when only vaguely formulated targets had been announced and bureaucratic rivalries prevented greater coordination. Second, the general orientation of the major economic categories is distinguished by the emphasis which is placed on consumer electronics. Given the fact that consumer electronics has potentially the largest market in China, the leadership in Beijing has ostensibly recognized that, given the current price structure and tax system, this shift will allow for the realization of benefits for both the society and the state. Also, in view of the fact that 70 to 80 percent of China's components production now goes into consumer electronics, Chinese planners hope that the components sector too will positively be affected by the shift to consumer electronics.[27]

Third, the set-up of a few key regional high technology centers, mainly in the coastal areas—Shanghai, Jiangsu province (Nanjing and Wuxi),

Table 3-3. Development Goals for China's Electronics in
the Seventh Five Year Plan (1986-1990)

Overall: Focus on *consumer electronics* as the largest market. Application
of *industrial electronic products*, notably in traditional industries; emphasis
on development of software, systems engineering, and consultant services.
Emphasis of *components development* on consumer electronics needs; other
areas include telecommunications, computers, instruments and military electronics. Priority also on measuring instruments, special technology equipment and special materials. Strengthening of *military electronics*; technology
transfer into civilian sector to be continued.

Gross production value: In 1990 share of 3.7 percent of national industrial
and agricultural GPV. Annual growth rate of 16 percent.

Regional policy: Focus on a few technologically advanced regions, especially
in *East China.*

Large project areas: Integrated circuits; enlargement of domestic technological
capabilities in color TVs and related picture tubes; *computers and telecommunications; electronic products for exports* (not specified).

Emphasis on five *techniques: Large-scale production* (focus: computer-aided
design [CAD], computer-aided manufacturing [CAM], computer-aided testing [CAT]); *miniaturized processing* (VLSI, 1-2 micrometers line width);
telecommunications (digitalization and switching); *industry-oriented electronics* (technical transformation of traditional industries); military *electronics.*

Organization: Establishment of *branch development centers* for microelectronics, computer software, telecommunications, industry-oriented electronics and military electronics. Set-up of more than *ten export bases.* Structural
reforms (divestment) to be continued.

Guangdong province, and Beijing—confirms the definitive departure from
the old strategy of establishing fully self-sufficient regional systems
throughout the country. Given the importance of the electronics industry
for China's future modernization, linking various regional activities into
a comprehensive sectoral policy indicates that the widening of regional
disparities is seen as an acceptable, and maybe necessary, part of the
development process. The advantages of such a policy can be seen in
the creation of a better structural environment to catch up with the industrialized countries. In addition, the planners hope that the interregional
gaps and specialization will also stimulate China's backward areas to
embark on a development trajectory that will allow them to approach
the level of the advanced regions in a reasonable length of time.[28]

SECTORAL ANALYSIS OF THE ELECTRONICS INDUSTRY

Integrated Circuits

Among the various subsectors within the electronics industry, integrated circuit (IC) research and production has received the greatest attention. The reason that this area has attracted such high-level interest has to do with several factors, the three most critical being the importance of integrated circuits to weapons-related development, the growing attention being given to a wide range of consumer electronics products, and the critical role that these components play in computer design and production. In some respects, the Chinese see ICs as a magic key that will allow them to overcome their problems of reliability and lack of flexibility as well as make possible reductions in the size, cost, and power requirements of various end-items.

There are approximately thirteen key facilities for manufacturing integrated circuits along with eight major research institutes. (See Table 3–4.) Total workers and staff number about 40,000, of which about 5,000 are engineers and technicians. Because of the significance attached to the development of ICs, they have begun to represent a growing, though still small, proportion of total electronics production. The total quantity of IC production in 1985 exceeded 53 million units, an over 100 percent increase over the 23.61 million units produced in 1983.[29] Due to excessive imports, IC production dropped by 15 percent from 1985 to 1986, to 46 million pieces, but climbed once again in 1987 to 78 million units. There also were steady improvements in chip quality, reliability and sophistication.[30] Similar gains were made in the production of discrete semiconductor devices, which increased from 734.21 million in 1983 to over 1.30 billion units in 1985. At present, the *China Daily* claims that there are 30 different categories and 680 types of ICs in serial production. In most instances, the level of the Chinese state of the art is late 1960s or 1970s vintage—though claims have been made that the manufacturing technologies for ICs in the 5 micron, 3 inch range have been mastered during the Sixth Five-Year Plan.[31] (See Table 3–5.) China's IC facilities currently produce linear, small-scale ICs (SSI), medium-scale ICs (MSI), and some large-scale ICs (LSI), including NMOS, PMOS, and CMOS. Within LSI technology, they have mastered 1K and 4K random access memory (RAM) and are in the process of perfecting their capabilities to manufacture 8-bit microprocessors and 16K RAM microcircuits. They

Table 3-4. Key IC R&D and Production Facilities in China.

Name	Location
A. Manufacturing	
Jiangnan Semiconductor Factory	Wuxi, Jiangsu
Tianguang Electronics Factory	Qinan, Gansu
Dongguang 878 Factory	Beijing
Changzhou Semiconductor Factory	Changzhou, Jiangsu Province
Beijing Semiconductor #2	Beijing
Beijing Semiconductor #3	Beijing
Shaoxing Electronics Factory	Shaoxing, Zhejiang Province
Shanghai #5 Components Factory	Shanghai
Shanghai #14 Radio Factory	Shanghai
Shanghai #19 Radio Factory	Shanghai
CAS Factory #109	Beijing
Lishan Microelectronics Corporation	Xian
Tianjin Semiconductor Factory	Tianjin
B. Research and Development	
Institute of Semiconductors, CAS	Beijing
Institute of Microelectronics, Qinghua U	Beijing
Institute of Metallurgy, CAS	Shanghai
Institute of Microelectronics, Fudan U	Shanghai
Solid State Research Institute, MEI (#24)	Sichuan
Nanjing Solid State Device Research Institute	Nanjing
Hebei Semiconductor Research Institute	Shijiazhuang, Hebei Province
Shenyang Liaohe Experimental Institute (#47)	Shenyang, Liaoning Province

Source: *Yearbook of China's Machine-Building and Electronics Industries, 1986.*

also produce some ECL and microwave semiconductor circuits—both of which approximate prevailing international standards.

Most designs tend to be based on American or Japanese technology.[32] China's CMOS technology appears to have come from RCA and Motorola designs, its HTL circuits are derived from Toshiba, and its ECL designs have been based on Motorola's ECL series. Copies of foreign microprocessor devices, such as the Intel 8080A and the Motorola 6800, have also been produced in China. While there is some

Table 3-5. Comparison of International and Chinese
Technological Development of Memory Chips.

| | International Level/China | | |
Year	Integration Density (bit)	Line Width (microns)	Wafer Size (inches)
1970	256	10	2
1973	1K	10	3
1975	4K / 1K	7	4
1977	16K	5	4
1979	64K / 4K	3	5
1981	/ 16K	/ 5	
1983	256K	2	6
1984	/ 64K		
1985	1024K / 64K	1–1.5 / 4–5	6 / 3–4
1986	4096K / 64K	0.5–1.0 / 3–4	6–8 / 3–4

Sources: International level: Guo Pingxin, "The Development of Microelectronics and the Emergence of Bio-Microelectronics," *Guide to China's Computer Industry* (Beijing: Electronics Industry Publishing House, 1985), pp. 115–123. Chinese level: Compiled from various Chinese sources.

basic design work being conducted in places such as the Institute of Semiconductors in Beijing and several of the previously mentioned institutes and universities, this is mostly geared to prototype development or specialized R&D for the defense sector.

It is clear that the demand for high-quality, reliable ICs in China greatly outstrips the supply.[33] According to China's National Semiconductor Physical-Chemical Analysis Center, the industry is plagued by a low-yield production rate, unstable quality, resultant high expenses and operating costs, and extreme waste of manpower and materials. Many factories still use manual processes to print circuits in the 10–15 micron range. Western visitors report that Chinese mask-making techniques are fairly satisfactory for the 6–8 micron range, but experience problems when they move into the 3–5 micron range. Most devices tend to be processed on 1.5–2.0 inch wafers, with only limited use of 3.0 inch wafers.[34] Of the 53 million ICs produced in 1985, medium (MSI) and large-scale (LSI) ICs accounted for only 4.0 percent of total production.[35] In addition, clean room facilities tend to be inadequate, which along with other shortcomings in quality control contributes to reduced yields. Recognition of the gap between the state of the art in the West and China has led the Chinese to seek large quantities of IC design and production equipment from abroad, especially from Japan and France. As a result, IC production facilities such as the Japanese-imported Jiangnan Plant in Wuxi (Jiangsu), ostensibly to support color TV production, are considered of vital importance.

On the R&D side, the State Science and Technology Commission has been mobilizing national resources and stressing greater cooperation regarding development and manufacture of large-scale integrated circuits.[36] One major objective of the SSTC has been to foster greater vertical integration in this subsector. For example, the Ministry of Metallurgy is being encouraged to meet the need for single crystal high-quality silicon, while the Ministry of Chemical Industry has been asked to provide super-purity reagents and high-purity air. In addition, the former State Machine-Building Commission and the MEI are attempting to work together in pursuit of more efficient production techniques and equipment—though in the area of automotive electronics, for example, they have yet to work out a well coordinated plan of action. Relatedly, in December 1982 at the Third National LSI Development, Vice-Premier Wan Li announced an eight-year program for LSI development that would concentrate on a "chain" containing four parts: scientific research, to technology exploitation, to industrial production, to wider application of LSI.[37] (See Table 3–6.)

Consumer Electronics

One of the results of China's increased emphasis on improving the incomes of rural and urban residents has been an increased demand for consumer electronics products. By the end of 1984 there were eighty-two black and white and five to six color TVs for every hundred urban households, and about seven (mostly black and white) TVs for every hundred rural households.[38] (See Table 3–7.) The key items being sought span the range from washing machines to electric fans. In the past, although China's production of such items was not insignificant, it was not able to meet international standards for product reliability and mean-time-between-failure (MTBF) ratio. The current stress being placed on improvements in production quality has already begun to yield tangible results. For example, Chinese black and white TVs have increased their MTBF to over 15,000 hours.[39]

Table 3–6. China's Proposed Three-Stage IC Plan.

Phase One (1986–1990): Foundation-Laying Stage—Master 3-inch silicon chip and 3.5 micron processing precision—and begin work toward the 2.0 micron level. Also ensure that items such as 4K MOS RAM, 16K DRAM, 4K CMOS RAM, 8-bit and 16-bit microprocessors, 1,600–2,400 gate CMOS gate array logic circuits, and low power TTL Schottky can be mass-produced. Development work should focus on 2 micron technology and CMOS circuits.

Phase Two (1991–1995): Continuing Development Stage—Continue to focus on LSI circuit production capability, mastering 4-inch silicon chips and 2 micron technology. Bring about large volume production of 64K MOS RAM and 6,400–12,800 gate CMOS arrays. Continue to concentrate on 16-bit microprocessors with some work on 32-bit processors and 256K MOS RAM. Also begin work on GaAs circuits. R&D work should focus on 5-inch, 1 micron technology.

Phase Three (1996–2000): Production of VLSI Stage—Form VLSI production capability. Production capabilities should include ability to manufacture 256K and 512K MOS RAM and 32-bit microprocessors in large quantities. Also some production of 1 Mb memories. R&D work should be focused on new generation ICs, such as high TC value superconductors and bioelectronic circuits. During this phase China's IC industry should strive to attain the U.S. level of 1990.

Source: Wang Yangyuan, "Tantan wo guo jicheng dianu zai jiushi nianda yao dadao de jishu mubiao" (Discussion about the technical goals of China's industry in the 1990s), *China Computerworld*, no. 9 (May 3, 1984): 3.

The primary factor holding back more rapid development of the consumer electronics industry has been the poor quality of domestically made components. In addition, many factory managers have eschewed introducing new technologies because demand already exceeds supply

Table 3–7. Production of TVs and Tape Recorders (in million units).

Year	1981	1982	1983	1984	1985	1986
Televisions (B&W)	5.02	5.41	5.90	8.09	10.81	9.69
Televisions (color)	0.15	0.29	0.53	1.29	3.78	4.99
Tape Recorders	1.52	3.28	4.38	6.74	11.02	14.49
Radios	36.34	15.56	18.43	20.08	13.89	NA

Source: *Zhongguo Dianzi Gongye Nianjian 1986* (Beijing: Dianzi Gongye Chubanshe, 1987), p. IV-68; *China Market*, September 1987, pp. 10–11.

for the items being produced at present quality levels. As a means to acquire the technical capacity to overcome shortcomings, China has often imported production lines from the West or engaged in joint venture projects. The establishment of the Jiangnan Radio Equipment Factory in Wuxi to produce linear ICs (the technology and equipment of which are imported from Toshiba) is a good example of this strategy. Some of these efforts have also begun to add to indigenous capabilities. For example, an 850,000-unit capacity black and white television tube production plant was set up in Chengdu in Sichuan.[40] This is the first completely domestically built tube production facility in China.

China's goal of significantly expanding production of consumer electronics has led them to give electronics a high priority within the effort towards technical transformation of enterprises. Accordingly, the Chinese have sought foreign technical assistance and have developed close working ties with the Electronics Industry Association of Japan. Through discussions with the various member companies, the Chinese have entered into several agreements to introduce Japanese manufacturing technology and to secure Japanese assistance in improving plant layout, quality control techniques, scheduling, and overall management.[41] Such improvements will enable electronics factories to meet the increasingly strict product standards being imposed by the State Economic Commission and the MEI.

One major stimulus to the enhancement of the consumer electronics sector has been the forging of closer links between military and civilian production. Because of the better quality and larger quantity of technical and production resources in the defense sector, civilian units have often been able to capitalize on the availability of these assets. In 1987, so-called third line military factories manufactured an estimated 8 billion yuan worth of civilian products, a sizable percentage of which were consumer electronics items.[42] In some instances, military facilities hope to advance their own revenue-generating opportunities and will not willingly share their capabilities. On the whole, however, the directive from Beijing that such interaction should occur more frequently has resulted in an upgrading of the quality of electronics components and their related consumer end-products.

Computers

In total, China has 132 enterprises under MEI and local governments. Of these, 83 factories produce computers and associated products; 10

of these are considered key computer manufacturing plants; and 47 factories produce computer peripherals. There are also about 26 key research institutes and an assortment of subcontractor production facilities. Total employment is more than 85,000 people, with 13,200 engineers and technicians. The computer industry produces thirty different mainframe and minicomputer models and thirteen different microcomputers. In 1987, the gross production value amounted to 1.81 billion yuan, only 4.4 percent of the overall electronics production value. Heretofore, the most successful example of computer development appears to be the DJS-100 minicomputer series, which was cooperatively designed and manufactured in the mid-1970s by Qinghua University, the Institute of Computer Technology under the CAS, the Tianjin Wireless Technology Research Institute, and the Beijing #3 Computer Factory. Today, however, progress in the microcomputer area appears to indicate that China has reached its next state of computer development and popularization. This is evidenced by the popularity of the Great Wall 0520 series (made in Beijing) and the Donghai 0520 series (made in Shanghai).

The situation in China's computer industry has been an evolving one, heavily influenced by a combination of domestic political as well as technological and economic factors. Considerations of self-reliance and technological dependence have also played a role in the definition of an overall strategy, though great uncertainty has existed and will continue to exist regarding the balance between foreign imports and indigenous efforts. In early 1982, the Chinese leadership articulated a blueprint for computer development which would catapult China by 1990 to the same technological levels achieved in the advanced developed countries in the early 1980s.[43] This was a very ambitious target since most foreign experts have considered China's computer design and manufacturing capabilities to be seven to ten years behind those of the United States and Japan. Total computer output was designed to triple by 1990, reaching an annual production capacity of 1,800 large and medium computers *and* 40,000 micro and single board computers. Foreign technology, although assigned an important role in the strategy, was clearly viewed with a large dose of caution. According to one former MEI official, "our consistent policy is to rely on ourselves, and at the same time learn from the advanced technology of foreign countries. . . . if we blindly import[ed] computers, we would have to spend billions of dollars before widespread use of computers in China was achieved."[44]

At a February 1984 conference, the essential elements of the current computer development strategy began to take shape. Focusing on the last two years of the Sixth Five-Year Plan, Jiang Zemin, former Minister of the MEI (and currently CCP Party Secretary in Shanghai), stated the following objectives:

1.   . . . we will concentrate our efforts on building a technological basis for the microcomputer industry and raise our ability to produce complete equipment. We will energetically develop the production of 8-bit computers, 16-bit computers, and a general system for microcomputers to form several assembly and adjustment lines for microcomputers sets.

2.   . . . we will energetically raise the percentage of China-made components and parts used for manufacturing microcomputers and focus our attention on making China-made circuit boards.

3.   We will pay close attention to the construction of three computer industrial bases of north China, south China, and east China and to forming combined service bodies for computer research and production to create favorable conditions for rapidly developing the computer industry in the Seventh 5-Year Plan period.

4.   To develop the electronics industry, we should centralize financial and material resources, pay special attention to key points, . . . expand foreign economic exchanges, introduce advanced technology, and strive to raise our ability to stand on our own feet to blaze a new trail in the electronics industry.[45]

For the rest of the decade (1986 to 1990), China's strategy for developing its computer industry will continue to contain many, if not all, of the points spelled out in 1984. For the most part, China's primary focus is on the linking together of electronics and informatics development. As previously mentioned, the centrality of this thrust was established in January 1985 in a speech made by then Vice-Premier Li Peng.[46] According to Li, the "emphasis of development of the electronics industry will be shifted onto the course of developing microelectronics technology as the foundation and computer and telecommunications equipment as the main body." Li's speech is significant because it reflects the realization among the leadership of two key points. First, there is an integral link between the electronics, informatics, and communications industries—the latter two cannot develop without significant progress in the case of the former. Second, there must be a greater degree of synergy between indigenous programs and foreign imports.[47] These themes were repeated again by the Minister of the MEI in his announcement of the development goals for China's electronics industry in the

Seventh Five Year Plan as well as the establishment of four national computer bases in Beijing, Shanghai/Jiangsu, Shenyang, and Guangdong.[48]

The Chinese will continue to emphasize the development of microcomputers more than other types of computers. Microcomputers are regarded as the most suitable in terms of prevailing production capabilities and potential applications. Technologically, the Chinese have been able to develop and produce 8-bit and single board computers, many of which have been modelled upon existing Western machines. On a limited basis, they have also been able to develop and manufacture 16-bit microcomputers; here again, many of these machines resemble Western equivalents such as IBM's PC/XT and PC/AT. The Chinese have shifted away from importing almost all 8-bit machines and many types of 16-bit computers, since they are now able to produce varieties of both machines on their own. According to 1987 statistics, Chinese-made microcomputers now occupy a 67 percent share of the domestic market, up from 36 percent in 1981. By 1990, officials from the MEI anticipate that about 80 percent of China's microcomputer needs will be met by domestic suppliers.[49]

In the development of mainframe computers (and supercomputers), which experienced serious problems in the past, the industry's overall strategic orientation is now entering a recovery stage. This is best exemplified by the attention being given to the 757 computer (10 million operations per second [mips]) designed and produced by the Chinese Academy of Sciences *and* the Galaxy (100 mips)—the Chinese answer to the CRAY-1—designed and produced by the National Defense S&T University in Changsha, Hunan. A decision was made in late 1985 to designate Beijing, which was chosen over several other cities, including Shanghai, as a special site for mainframe computer development.[50] The basic design orientation—which has been dictated by considerations of standardization, software compatibility, and networking needs, will be to emulate Western models produced by such prominent firms as DEC, IBM, and Control Data Corporation.

While mainframe development will be given additional capital investment and support, it appears likely that the stress on development of microcomputers will continue during the rest of the 1980s, with increasing emphasis placed on domestic production of both components and complete machines. There is also some evidence of a growing interest in minicomputers because of their price-performance ratio compared to large mainframes. One driving force behind the concentration on microcomputers, and more recently minicomputers, is the shift away from stand-alone machines towards more networking both within and between organizations as well as the growing emphasis on application of computers in industrial, management, and office settings. (See Table 3–8.) At a national conference on computer application in June 1986, Lü Dong, minister-in-charge of the former State Economic Commission and vice-chairman of the State Council's Electronics Leading Group, announced that the machine-building and electronics industries were selected to experiment with computer management information systems and computer-assisted production during the 1986 to 1990 time frame.[51] In this regard, China hopes gradually, though steadily, to approach the current breadth of Western uses, quality levels, and processing capabilities by the 1990s.

The major constraints in establishing an advanced Chinese computer industry fall into four categories:

1. Manufacturing capabilities
2. Peripheral equipment
3. Technical personnel
4. Software

As indicated previously, techniques for mass production of final products and computer components are severely lacking in China. Even though advanced components are being developed in the laboratory, many factories lack the necessary production equipment and managerial know-how to produce these items in sufficient quantities and at necessary

Table 3–8. Microcomputer Applications, 1985.

Field of Application	Quantity	Percentage
Instrument and measurement	984	2.1
Process control	662	21.6
Management	306	10.0
CAD/CAM/CAE	267	8.7
Software development	264	8.6
Medicine and health	173	5.6
Chinese character processing	78	2.5
Optimization/Decision making	42	1.3
Other	296	9.6
Total (1985)	3,072	100.0
Total installed (overall)	217,900	

Source: Guo Pingxin, "China's Strategies for Computer Application," Paper presented to the Southeast Asian Computer Conference, Bangkok, November 1986.

reliability levels. A good example of how these shortcomings can affect the development of a specific machine involves the DJS-186, a 16-bit minicomputer similar to DEC's PDP-11 series. The DJS-186, whose development began in 1978, experienced numerous problems. First, the delivery of domestically made ICs did not materialize and imports had to be used instead; second, there was continued uncertainty over which factory was going to take over manufacture of the prototype.

The Chinese remain unable to meet the growing needs of computer users in most facets of peripherals, mainly because they are lacking in both technology and manufacturing capabilities. This is particularly true regarding items such as disk drives, printers, and monitors. For example, while places such as Taiwan and South Korea have been able to push forward on monitor development because of their achievements in televisions, China has not been able to rely on such a technological foundation to move ahead in this area.

While the Chinese have set out to train a substantially increased number of computer scientists, engineers, and programmers, they still do not have a broad-based pool of experts to support a full-fledged national effort throughout the country. Estimates are that China will need some 600,000 computer personnel by 1990, a target that will remain difficult to attain even with the ongoing improvement and expansion in computer education. According to one estimate by an official from the MEI's State Computer Administration, at least 100,000 trained specialists are needed in research and production and an additional 500,000 computer operators will be needed by the 1990s.

The Chinese appear to have made substantial progress in the development of Chinese character input systems and software. In mid-1985, a computerized Chinese-language information storage system was introduced by the Beijing Teachers University. It can automatically process any Chinese language information into corresponding key word and phrase data banks. And in late 1983, China's first computer-aided design (CAD) system for exterior car body design was produced through the joint effort of the Shanghai Tractor and Automobile Research Institute and the Institute of Mathematics at Fudan University.[52] In early 1986, China's first comprehensive software package, called "The Software Package for Modern Digital Signal Processing," was introduced by the Northern Jiaotong University in Xian in conjunction with five other institutes in Beijing, Shanghai, and Xian.[53] The package covers a total of forty-two programs ranging from measurement statistics to modern spectral analysis.

As in the past, the problem of portability continues to be widespread; a significant percentage of the software being developed still is machine-specific. In the past, software development was considered the Achilles' heel of Chinese computer development. Today, the several central government standards for software development and various organizations such as the China Software Corporation and the China Computer Users Association will help remedy many of these problems.[54] Moreover, building on its growing capabilities, China has started to become a source of software exports and development services in the international market.

Domestically, however, obstacles and some resistance to the introduction and expanded use of computers still remain. Even where computers have been acquired, underutilization remains a serious and widespread problem. The investment made in developing application systems is not commensurate with that made in developing or importing basic systems. According to an *EDP China* report, " . . . users are usually only willing to pay for hardware and hand out money almost grudgingly for software. The importance of researching and designing application systems is not yet widely recognized."[55] The problem is particularly acute regarding domestically made machines.

According to sources in Beijing, 32,000 microcomputers were manufactured in 1985, while there were still 40,000 stocked in warehouses with no customers in sight.[56] Officials in the computer industry have suggested that the utilization rate of installed microcomputers in Beijing municipality is only 26 percent, while the national average is in the range of 15 to 20 percent.[57] The problem of poor utilization has its roots in personnel shortages. Other key factors include organizational rivalry, intense bureaucratic jealousy, poor maintenance, limited software availability, and poor after-sales service.[58] One estimate suggests that the Chinese will waste between US$20–$85 million over the next three years because of improper use and maintenance of imported computers.[59]

Most important, however, the drive to introduce computers into industry and society has stimulated expanded interactions among component producers, computer manufacturers, and potential end-users. Given the frequent gap between developers and users in China, this trend could be highly significant. (See Table 3–9.) For example, the Shaoguan Radio Factory in Guangdong, which is a leading manufacturer of 8-bit and 16-bit microcomputers in South China, has transferred a number of its engineers and skilled workers to form an outreach/sales team to promote microcomputer use.[60] The factory has also instituted such measures as user training classes and a lecture series.

Table 3–9. Major Achievements of China's Computer Industry, 1977–1988.

1977	Development of China's first microcomputer (DJS-050)
1979	Development of HDS-9 (5 MIPS) by CAS Institute of Computer Technology
1980	Development of DJS-052 microprocessor (8-bit, one chip) by the Anhui Institute for Electronics Technology
1983	Development of China's first supercomputer, *Yinhe* (Galaxy), 100 MIPS, by the Changsha S&T University for National Defense
1983	Development of the 0520 microcomputer (IBM PC-compatible) by the MEI Institute No. 6
1983	Development of the 757 10 MIPS parallel computer by CAS Institute of Computer Technology
1983	Development of a 16-bit desktop computer (77-II) by the Lishan Microcomputer Corporation
1984	Development of the 16-bit TQ-0671 microcomputer system by the Tianjin Computer Institute (CPU: MC 6800)
1985	Development of NCI-AP 2701 floating point array processor by North China Institute of Computer Technology
1985	Development of NCI-2780 super-minicomputer (32-bit) by North China Institute of Computer Technology
1985	Development of 8030 computer by East China Institute of Computer Technology (compatible with IBM 370/138)
1985	Development of YH-X1 super-minicomputer by the Changsha S&T University for National Defense
1985	Development of YH-F1 emulator by the Changsha S&T University for National Defense
1985	Development of the TJ-82 image computer by Qinghua U
1986	Development of HN-2730 super-minicomputer (32-bit) by the CAS Shenyang Institute of Computer Technology and the Huanan Computer Corporation
1987	Development, production and marketing of new generation of microcomputers, 0530 series (286 and 386 models).
1988	Development of the S-8/20 distributed processing mini-computer system by the #706 Institute under the Ministry of Space Industry.

There has already been some interesting work done in the attempt to establish several nationwide economic and S&T information networks. According to comments made by Premier Li Peng, the Chinese intend to establish eleven national computerized information systems for such fields as telecommunications and weather forecasting during the Seventh FYP. There is also a program under way to establish an information network linked through the China National Science and Technology Center in Beijing.[61] Ten key coastal cities, along with the Institute for Scientific and Technical Information (ISTIC) under the SSTC, are involved.[62] The Chinese are attempting to draw upon Western data bases and to create their own data retrieval systems. Progress, however, has been impeded by China's poor communications infrastructure, which has added a large element of insecurity and unreliability into data transfer and computer communication. Recent improvements in communications, obtained primarily through technology and equipment imports, soon may help alleviate some of these problems. For the present, however, local area networks and distributed processing remain the exception rather than the rule.

Communications

China's communication system is one of the most serious weak links in its infrastructure.[63] China averages 0.53 telephones per hundred persons—by comparison, Western Europe has an average of 55 per hundred persons. To increase China's telephones to a modest five per hundred persons would require adding nearly 50 million telephones. Most of the equipment in place is analog with manual switching—though, through recent imports, noticeable improvements are occurring. The leadership has recognized the importance of communications in the Seventh FYP. Investment in communications of Renminbi (RMB) 10 billion yuan is planned, and the goal is to attain a 7 percent share of the country's gross value of agricultural and industrial output.[64] Major recipients of the investment will be Beijing, Tianjin, Shanghai, Guangdong, and several other coastal cities. Chinese plans project that by the year 2000 there will be 20 to 25 telephones per hundred persons in the major urban areas and an overall density of 2.8 per hundred persons nationwide. There is great interest in the use of microwave systems and optical fiber technology to modernize communication.

Primary responsibility for communications falls within the purview of both the MEI and the MPT. The MEI has 105 enterprises that compete with and at times complement the production enterprises managed by the MPT. MEI's range of telecommunications products includes telephones, switching equipment, facsimile apparatuses, microwave relay equipment, equipment for satellite ground stations and so on. Total MEI output in 1985 was RMB 28.6 billion yuan. The MPT has 135 enterprises, 29 of which are considered high-caliber facilities. Gross production value amounted to over RMB 10.0 billion yuan in 1985. MPT too produces a full range of telecommunications equipment; over the last two years several pieces of new equipment have been developed, including 34 megabits/sec digital multiplex equipment; 2,400 bits/sec modulator-demodulators, and 30 channel PCM (one way coding and decoding) terminals. There is also a Ministry of Broadcasting and TV (MBTV) that engages in the manufacture of broadcasting and television installations. The MBTV has fifty-two manufacturing enterprises, eight directly under the ministry and forty-four under local administration. Typical products include installations for recording, transmitting, and control of broadcasting; audio amplifiers; and magnetic tapes.

As is generally the case when there are similarities in production and overlapping interests, there is intense rivalry among those organizations to protect their turf. The problems are compounded by the fact that there is also a great coordination problem between the local posts and telecommunications bureaus and the MPT, with the former trying to maintain independence of action and autonomy regarding potential foreign partners and the latter eager to establish national standards and create a nationally linked, efficient communications system.

China appears to have particular interest in mobile communication technologies.[65] Some of the impetus for the focus on mobile communications derives from military applications. For example, the Chinese have paid close attention to the development of the triforces tactical communication system in the U.S. Yet, as many aspects of the modernization program advance, a need for all sorts of civilian-based mobile telecommunications capabilities has emerged. Among the key applications for China are: command stations for offshore drilling platforms and supply entities; daily response to abnormal phenomena, such as natural disaster; law enforcement; general business communications, e.g. sales; and paging.

NOTES

1. Wilson Dizard, *The Coming Information Age* (New York: Longman, 1982). See also Thomas Forester, ed., *The Information Technology Revolution* (Cambridge, Mass.: MIT Press, 1985).

2. Thomas Forester, ed., *The Microelectronics Revolution* (Cambridge, Mass.: MIT Press, 1980).

3. According to a report by the Club of Rome,

> the promise of the microprocessor is that through its ubiquitous applications in the automation of industry and the tertiary sector, it is capable of increasing productivity to the extent that it should be possible to provide all the resources required by any country, including those of defense, health, education, nourishment and welfare, to provide a reasonably high material standard of living for everyone, without depleting or degrading the resources of the plant, with only a fraction of the physical work expended today.

See Günter Friedrichs and Adam Schaff, eds., *Microelectronics and Society: A Report to the Club of Rome* (New York: Mentor, 1982). See also Nathan Rosenberg and L.E. Birdzell, *How the West Grew Rich* (New York: Basic Books, 1986).

4. Michael J. Piore and Charles Sabel, *The Second Industrial Divide* (New York: Basic Books, 1984).

5. Michael Dertouzos and Joel Moses, eds., *The Computer Age: A Twenty Year View* (Cambridge, Mass.: MIT Press, 1979).

6. Gene Gregory, *Japanese Electronics Technology: Enterprise and Innovation* (Tokyo: Japan Times Press, 1985).

7. Francis Rushing and Carole Brown, eds., *National Policies for Developing High Technology Industries* (Boulder, Colo.: Westview Press, 1986).

8. Hans Kühner: *Die Chinesische Akademie der Wissenschaftern und ihre Vorläufer 1928–1985* (Hamburg: Mitteilungen des Instituts für Asienkunde, no. 146, 1986).

9. Manfredo Macioti: "Scientists Go barefoot," *Successo,* January 1971, quoted in Jon Sigurdson, *Technology and Science in the People's Republic of China* (Oxford, Pergamon Press, 1980), p.38.

10. According to Cheng Chu-yuan's study of China's machine-building industry, "the technology of electronics, which has made great strides since 1958, was first of all to satisfy the demands of national defense." See Cheng Chu-yuan, *The Machine-Building Industry in Communist China* (Chicago: Aldine Publishers, 1971).

11. According to one source in Shanghai, prior to the post-Mao economic reforms, military factories produced on a "cost plus 5 percent" basis, with the achievement of the tasks always superceding considerations of economic efficiency and cost.

12. Xiu, Jinya, "De li tuijin dianzi jisuanji de yanjiu, shengchan he yingyong gongzuo" (Push vigorously the research, production and application of computers), Jingji Guanli, no. 2, (1984): 12–15.

13. Jon Sigurdson: "Technology and Sciences—Some Issues in China's Modernization," in U.S. Congress, Joint Economic Committee, *Chinese Economy Post-Mao*, (Washington, D.C.: Government Printing Office, 1978), vol. 1, pp. 476–534, especially pp. 519–524.

14. It is still very difficult to identify the key players in the debate as well as the substantive issues, if any, that were actually the object of disagreement. Speculation is that is was probably Marshal Nie Rongzhen, then head of the National Defense Science and Technology Commission (NDSTC), who came under attack by the radical faction within the central leadership for "taking electronics as the core." Underlying this political attack might have been the fact the Nie was instrumental in trying to insulate the electronics industry from the political struggles initiated by the "Red Guards." In 1968, most of China's major electronics facilities were placed under the direct supervision of the NDSTC, thereby effectively placing the electronics industry outside of the possible control of the radical faction. During this time, personnel working in these facilities wore Peoples' Liberation Army uniforms and took most of their tasking from the Chinese military establishment. After the turbulence of the Cultural Revolution and its aftermath subsided, some percentage of these units (the precise quantity remains still unknown) were returned to their civilian status.

15. For details of this divestment effort see *China Daily*, August 2, 1985 and May 9, 1986.

16. "New Computer Giant Eyes Home Market," *Beijing Review*, January 19, 1987, pp. 5–6.

17. These are (1) the Jiangnan Semiconductor Equipment Factory (also known as MEI State Factory #742) in Wuxi, and (2) the Shaanxi Color Television Tube Factory (also known as MEI State Factory #4400) in Xianyang.

18. The principle of "dual leadership" may also apply to enterprises that are jointly administered by provinces and cities or cities and counties. In addition, it is also possible for a combination of such "local" entities along with a central government ministry to administer an enterprise, e.g. city, province and the ministry. A good example of the latter is the "Zijin Information Industry Corporation" in Nanjing.

19. Personal interviews in Beijing, January 1986.

20. Li Peng, "Dianzi he xinxi change yao wei si hua jianshe fuwu" (The electronics and information industries should serve the construction of the four modernizations), *Jingji Ribao*, January 14, 1985.

21. Jonathan Pollack, *The Chinese Electronics Industry in Transition*, A Rand Note, N-2306 (Santa Monica, Calif.: Rand Corporation, May 1985), p. 21.

22. *Jixie Zhoubao* (Machine-Building Weekly), no. 149 (July 29, 1983): 2.

23. Fang Yi, "Zai quan guo kexue jishu da hui shang de baogao [zhaiyao]" (Report at the National Science Conference [Extracts]), *Renmin Ribao,* March 29, 1978.
24. *Renmin Ribao,* August 12, 1971.
25. See Li Peng, "The electronics industry should serve the four modernizations" and *Xinhua,* January 11, 1985 in *Foreign Broadcast Information Service—China,* January 15, 1985, pp. K25–27.
26. Li Tieying, "Jianchi gaige, jiasu fazhan, nuli zhenxing dianzi gongye" (Continue the reform, speed up the development, actively invigorate the electronics industry," *Zhongguo Dianzi Bao,* no. 59 (January 21, 1986).
27. In this context it might be useful to study the experiences of 1981–82 when there was a similar approach to take consumer electronics as the key area of China's electronics industry. Given the numerous technological and manufacturing problems which still exist one may conclude that the focus on consumer electronics had only marginal positive effects on the development of the components sector. Of course, there is a number of other factors which explain the problems in China's semiconductor area. See Simon and Rehn, "Innovation in China's Semiconductor Components Industry: The Case of Shanghai."
28. Chen Jiyuan, "Diqu jingji jiegou duice" (Measures regarding the regional economic structure), in Sun Shangqing, ed., *Lun jingji jiegou duice* (On measures regarding the economic structure) (Beijing: Chinese Academy of Social Sciences Publishing House, 1984), pp. 318–360.
29. *Zhongguo Kexue Jishu Zhengce Zhinan* (Primer on China's S&T Policy) (Beijing: S&T Publishing House, 1986), p. 137. By 1990, China hopes to produce 400 million ICs per year.
30. "Nation Revives Integrated Circuit Industry and Reduces Imports," *China Daily,* Business Weekly, July 26, 1987, p.1.
31. Xu Daorong, " 'Liu Wu' qijian dianzi keji gongguan chengji xianzhu" (Remarkable electronics S&T breakthroughs in the sixth five-year plan), *Zhongguo Dianzi Bao,* no. 101 (June 17, 1986): 3.
32. Sun Tingcai, "Qian tan weixingji de xuanze" (A discussion about the selection of microcomputers), *Dianzi Jishu* (Electronic Technology), no. 7 (1982): 5–8.
33. Chinese officials, led by Vice-Premier Li Peng, believe that massive imports of ICs have seriously injured the domestic IC industry. In 1985, for example, estimates were that China would need a total of 170 million ICs, but close to 200 million pieces were imported. At the same time, over 52 million pieces were domestically produced, creating an excess of nearly 85 million. Foreign ICs tend to get used first unless other instructions come from above.
34. According to a March 1986 report, China's immediate goal is to develop 3 micron technology for mass production while continuing research on one-micron technologies.

35. These capabilities correspond to the US manufacturing level of 1967 and the Japanese manufacturing level of 1969. See *Zhongguo Kexue Jishu Zhengce Zhinan.*

36. In late 1985, Qinghua University received certification for production of China's first 16K static RAM, which measured 28 square millimeters, was 0.003 mm thick, and contained 108,000 transistors and other devices. In addition, a 64K NMOS DRAM was also developed by MEI Institute #24 and the Jiangnan Radio Factory in Wuxi. The chip, whose size and 3.96 × 7.56 square mm, contained 150,000 elements and attained a minimum line width of 2.5 microns. Finally, in September 1986 the completion of a 16 bit CPU developed by the CAS Shanghai Institute of Metallurgy in cooperation with the MSI Lishan Microelectronics Corporation and the Shanghai Jiaotong University was announced. *Guoji Dianzi Bao,* June 11, 1986 and September 11, 1986.

37. Currently, the Chinese are working with X-ray lithography in order to move ahead into VLSI technology. Some of this work is being carried out at the Institute of Semiconductors under the CAS, a facility that was recently completely refurbished and imported a number of pieces of new testing and manufacturing equipment from Japan.

38. State Statistical Bureau, ed., *Statistical Yearbook of China 1985* (Beijing: China Statistics Publishing House, 1985), pp. 565 and 573.

39. "Electronics Industry Booming," *China Daily,* March 6, 1986, p. 4.

40. "Chengdu shi dianzi gongye qunian chuang lishi zui hao shuiping" (Last year, Chengdu's electronics industry realized the best level in history), *Zhongguo Dianzi Bao,* March 21, 1986, p. 1.

41. For a Japanese assessment of China's electronics industry see Yoshio Nishimura, "China Heads Towards the Silicon Age," *Nikkei Electronics,* no. 412 (January 12, 1987): 267–282.

42. "Military Plants Turn to Civilian Production," *China Daily,* January 7, 1988, p. 1.

43. The description of these goals was provided by Li Rui, former general manager of the department of computer industry under the MEI. See "Computers in China," *Summary of World Broadcast/Far East* (FE/W1201/A/13), November 10, 1982, pp. 13–14.

44. Ibid., p. 14.

45. "Minister Jiang Zemin on China's Developing Electronics Computer Industry," *Zhongguo Xinwen She,* February 21, 1984, translated in *Foreign Broadcast Information Service—People's Rep;ublic of China,* February 28, 1984, pp. K8–9.

46. Li Peng, "The Electronics and Information Industries Should Serve the Four Modernizations."

47. For an earlier commentary on this latter point see Ge Zhangyi, "A Discussion of the Countermeasures of the World's New Technological Revolution," *Guoji Maoyi Wenti*, September–October 1984, pp. 6–10.

48. Li Tieying, "Continue the Reform, Speed Up the Development, Actively Invigorate the Electronics Industry."

49. Xiu, "Push Vigorously the Domestic Production of Microcomputers During the Seventh Five-Year Plan."

50. "Beijing Area Chosen to Manufacture Mainframe and Medium-Scale Computers," *EDP China Report* 4 (November 30, 1985): 18.

51. Lü Dong, "Zai quan guo jisuanji yingyong gongzuo huiyi shang de baogao (zhaiyao)" "Report at the National Work Conference for Computer Applications." [Extracts]. *Zhongguo Keji Bao*, no. 75 (June 25, 1986): 2.

52. "China's First CAD System for Car Body," *Jiefang Ribao*, October 20, 1983, p. 2, translated in *Joint Publications Research Service—China Science and Technology 85-038*, November 5, 1985, p. 68.

53. "Software and Money Aid Science," *China Daily*, April 11, 1986.

54. A good example of Chinese progress was the recent development of HC-DOS, a Chinese-English operating system that runs on the IBM 5550. The 5550 is a multi-function microcomputer that can handle Chinese character inputs. The operating system was developed by the Institute of Computer Applications Research at Hunan University and a computer company in Changsha. All of the original software for the IBM PC and the 5550 can still operate using HC-DOS.

55. *EDP China Report* (June 17, 1986): 242.

56. "Computers Facing Glut in Market," *China Daily*, January 11, 1986.

57. Ibid. According to one source, a survey of 14,000 microcomputers in place in Beijing revealed that most are used less than three hours of day. "Beijing Has Future as Computer Capital," *China Daily*, January 18, 1986, p. 2.

58. There are approximately only 10,000 people involved in computer services in China. The creation of the China Computer Services Corporation in 1984 is a positive step toward improving computer usage, though the numbers of people and their skill levels remain inadequate. See Chen Liwei, "The Position and the Role of Computer Services in the Computer Industry," *Dianzi Xuebao*, no. 5 (September 1984): 65–67, translated in *Joint Publications Research Service—China Science and Technology 85-009*, April 9, 1985, pp. 57–61.

59. Sam Howe, "China's High Tech Troubles," *New York Times*, May 5, 1985, p. F9.

60. *Nanfang Ribao*, March 4, 1984, p. 2, translated in *Joint Publications Research Service—China Science and Technology 85-014*, May 2, 1985, pp. 40–41.

61. "Information Center Construction Starts," *China Daily*, September 24, 1984, p. 3.
62. According to Wang Tingjiong, director of ISTIC, there are more than 60,000 people engaged in information collection, dissemination, and services. *China Daily*, April 2, 1986.
63. For a general overview of the situation in the telecommunications sector see "A Facelift for Telecommunications," *Intertrade*, no. 2 (1985): 9–18.
64. "Investments in Post and Telecommunications to Rise" *China Daily*, September 4, 1985, p. 2.
65. He Siyi, "Give Full Play to the Role of Mobile Telecommunications in China's Four Modernizations' Drive," *Dianzi Xuebao*, no. 4 (1983): 37–43.

4 IMPLEMENTING THE DEVELOPMENT STRATEGIES FOR CHINA'S ELECTRONICS INDUSTRY
The Case of Shanghai

Generally speaking, Shanghai has played a strategic role in China's industrial and technological development. In the early 1980s, for example, approximately one-ninth of the country's entire industrial output, one-sixth of the central government's revenues, one-sixth of the central government's revenues, and one-sixth of China's total exports came from Shanghai. Shanghai's per capita income, which equalled over US $1,000 in 1985, was over three times the national average. Moreover, the municipality possesses a comparatively strong science and technology base, with 71 research institutes, 108 S&T associations, and about 55,000 S&T personnel and 400,000 technicians. In addition, Shanghai is the site of several dynamic universities—Fudan, Jiaotong and Shanghai S&T —all three of which have substantially contributed to the creation of an active research and education environment.

Shanghai's industrial base also holds a comparatively strong position within China's overall industrial structure. In 1986, the gross value of industrial output in Shanghai amounted to RMB 87.09 billion yuan, which equalled about 7.8 percent of the total value of the country's industrial output. Within this category, light industry (RMB 47.81 billion) accounted for 9.0 percent of China's light industrial output and heavy industry (RMB 39.28 billion) accounted for 6.7 percent of China's heavy industrial output. Similarly, the municipality's electronics industry has also performed quite well in recent years, especially in terms of product quality and diversity. In 1985, the gross production value of Shanghai's electronics sector amounted to RMB 4.73 billion yuan, 15.9 percent of the national total. Shanghai plays a particularly significant role with respect to consumer electronics. In 1986 Shanghai accounted for 23.6 percent of China's entire TV production, 20.6 percent of cassette recorder production, and 14.4 percent of washing machine production.[1]

Shanghai's rather well-developed industrial and technological base will help it play an important role in the present and future modernization of China's electronics industry. However, the statistics obscure a number of fundamental weaknesses in Shanghai's economy, including:

1. Outdated plants and equipment. About half of Shanghai's industrial equipment dates from the 1930s and 1940s, nearly one-third is from the 1950s, only about 11.0 percent is from the 1960s and 1970s, and only a very small percentage is from the 1980s.[2]

2. Low skills levels among workers and staff, resulting in low labor productivity. The average technical level of Shanghai's workers dropped from Grade-4 before the Cultural Revolution to Grade 2.5. In the city's Bureau of Instruments, technicians dropped from 17 percent of the total number of employees in 1965 to only 9.2 percent in 1983.[3]

3. Poorly developed links between S&T and production. Many achievements in the research sector stop at the gift, sample, and exhibit level.

4. Inadequate management capabilities. In the early 1980s a survey of more than 1,800 state-run factories revealed that 57 percent did not possess adequate managerial records, 38.2 percent had inadequate control over raw material quotes, and 47.7 percent had incomplete personnel records.[4]

5. Poor overall product quality. While some neighboring provinces have been concerned with improving product quality and sophistication, quite a few of Shanghai's products have lost market share and "have become less popular because they remain at the 'grandmother's age' stage of development."[5] Moreover, Shanghai's available capital has been declining as revenues have not kept up with expenditures. This situation has precluded new investment in many badly needed infrastructure projects. (See Figure 4-1.)

Figure 4-1. Shanghai in Comparative Perspective: Year-to-Percent Change in Industrial Output.

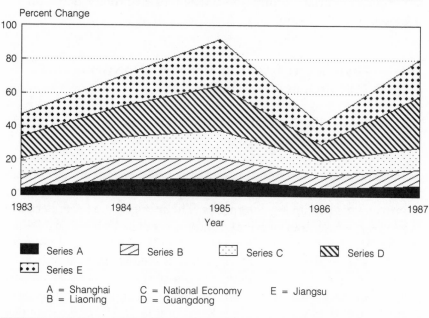

Source: Louise do Rosair, "Red Light, Green Light," Far Eastern Economic Review (April 21, 1988): 70.

The increasing weight of these factors has been a major impetus for igniting the debate on the future course of Shanghai's development and its integration into the overall national modernization program. In this context, the further development of a modern, technologically advanced electronics industry has been viewed as an answer to Shanghai's economic woes. By shifting away from its traditional orientation—reliance on capital- and labor-intensive industries—toward more skill- and knowledge-intensive industries and service (tertiary) industries, Shanghai officials hope to re-establish its prominence as China's leading technological, economic, and commercial center.[6]

The chapter takes a microlevel view of how the various elements of China's overall electronics strategy have been interpreted and implemented in Shanghai. It analyzes the interactions between the central government and Shanghai authorities in order to highlight some of the essential tensions involved in the move towards greater decentralization in China. It discusses the details of Shanghai's own production and research situation and examines the various methods adopted by Shanghai officials to launch their own electronics drive. Finally, it assesses the impact of recent reforms on Shanghai's electronics development potential.

HISTORICAL BACKGROUND OF SHANGHAI'S ELECTRONICS INDUSTRY

Laying the Foundation for the Electronics Industry, 1956–1978

At the time of the Communist takeover in 1949, Shanghai's electronics industry proper consisted of only a few repair shops and a small number of instruments-producing enterprises. The strongest area was electrical machinery, which had developed during the late 1930s and 1940s.[7] During the First Five Year Plan (1953–1957), Shanghai followed the guidelines set at the national level, which aimed at establishing an indigenous Chinese machine-building industry and a number of new factories in this sector. Within this framework, a number of new electronics enterprises were founded. For example, in 1952 the Shanghai Broadcast Equipment Factory was founded; it has turned out to be one of Shanghai's major producers of consumer electronics and (military-directed) telecommunications equipment.[8] Since the electronics industry was organizationally a part of the machine-building sector, the extent of production and research activities which were exclusively devoted to electronics is difficult to identify.

After 1956, the outlines of a formal electronics industry in Shanghai began to take shape. Due to its traditionally important position within the Chinese technological and economic system, Shanghai has been regarded as a major actor in the national R&D programs. For example, with respect to the electronics targets contained in the National Science Plan of 1956, both Beijing and Shanghai were viewed as focal points for achieving major technological breakthroughs. Gradually, through the allocation of investment funds and personnel, Shanghai established itself as one of China's most advanced industrial and technological centers. A number of new research institutes were founded during this period; these became the backbone of the fledgling electronics industry. In addition, Shanghai became involved in many of the research projects that were to become the cutting edge of China's electronic technology.[9] While there were clear benefits from being in the forefront of electronics development, there were also a number of shortcomings. Most important, a feeling of technological superiority emerged in Shanghai's research sector; as a result, a disproportionate amount of time was spent maintaining this leadership at the expense of addressing the more pressing problem of creating a well-structured, responsive manufacturing base.

Nonetheless, Shanghai was in some respects ahead of the general pace of electronics development in other parts of the country, especially in recognizing the potential significance of electronics. For example, Shanghai began R&D efforts on integrated circuit technology as early as 1964 and 1965. Since the technological importance of ICs was not fully comprehended at the central level, the development of China's first IC in 1965 did not attract widespread national attention and remained a local project. As a local project, it received little direct nurturing from above. One consequence of the lack of explicit application targets for ICs during their initial phase of development was that mass production of these new components did not take place. Only after the Chinese military learned about the importance of using ICs in advanced weapons systems were central direction and support given to Shanghai's further IC efforts.[10]

Another important factor shaping the establishment of Shanghai's electronics industry was China's financial system. The logic of China's financial system required that Shanghai, as the country's economic center, had to transfer the bulk of its financial revenues to the central government. The central government used such monies to finance economic construction, especially in the hinterland areas.[11] Shanghai proper received only a small portion of the revenues it took in. Hence, the development of Shanghai's electronics industry, among others, was mainly financed through local funds.[12] This meant that with respect to the creation of a production base there was only limited financial support by the central government.

The development pattern of the Shanghai electronics industry was apparently typical of the course of electronics development in other sections of China. Due to the overall lack of ample materials, funding, and competent personnel to support a new industry, it was mainly the textile and the light industry sectors which provided the workers and workshops needed for the newly established electronics enterprises.[13] It is difficult to know whether this pattern applies to all of the new electronics enterprises in Shanghai and elsewhere, but it is likely that this pattern was replicated given the industry's economic role and the paucity of material and financial resources during its early development years.[14]

One can better appreciate the relationship between the central government in Beijing and Shanghai by looking at the competition between the two entities. After the electronics industry in Shanghai had exhibited its technological and economic strengths, the Fourth Ministry of Machine-Building (MEI), now the MMBEI, tried to acquire control of a number of Shanghai's key electronics enterprises and place them under its administration. The municipality refused to accede to what in reality constituted a grab for resources by the MEI.[15] This fact might explain, to some extent, the frequently strained relations between the Ministry and the municipality until recent times.

The problems that emerged during the industrial development in China between 1956 and 1978 are also visible in Shanghai's electronics industry. The adoption of a Soviet-type economic structure in Shanghai resulted in serious vertical barriers between research and production. Moreover, as with the electronics industry in general, Shanghai's electronics production structure showed a certain bias towards satisfying military demand. In the early 1970s, even though more widespread computer applications were encouraged and a shift towards minicomputers was regarded as necessary for future economic development, a substantial breakthrough did not occur in Shanghai because its computer R&D and manufacturing structure were oriented towards developing large machines, achieving high processing speeds, and creating large computer memories.[16] It was only after Shanghai's computer industry almost collapsed in the early 1980s that measures to reform the system were discussed and introduced.[17]

The Period of Readjustment 1978–1985

With the onset of the four modernizations program in 1978, Shanghai's electronics industry developed an even greater degree of momentum. Here again, the differences in the perspectives between the central government and the local Shanghai government revealed themselves. On the one hand, central government leaders in Beijing began to recognize the potential contribution that Shanghai could make to overall electronics development. On the other hand, local Shanghai leaders were not certain of the precise role that electronics should play in Shanghai's overall development strategy. While the importance of electronics was generally recognized, the notion of taking high technology as the core of Shanghai's development was not well received by a large number of influential individuals, many of whom were concerned about the future status of so-called traditional industries in Shanghai. Thus, two sets of debates emerged, one between Beijing in its role as the central government and Shanghai, and one within Shanghai itself.

Between 1979 and 1981, the basis for the development of Shanghai's electronics industry was a series of vaguely formulated guidelines set at the national level by the former MEI. As had been the case since 1949, Beijing's focus was on getting more output from Shanghai's existing manufacturing capacity. In other words, the central authorities perceived Shanghai primarily not as a catalyst to overall electronics development, but rather as a key supplier of basic electronic products. In research and development, Beijing also saw Shanghai playing an important role but at the same time sought to take advantage of its existing strengths. The overall problem for Beijing, in many respects, was that it did not want to see the workhouse of its economy falter as a result of the problems it was experiencing—and at the same time, Beijing was unwilling to provide substantial direct support or allow Shanghai the freedom to proceed in its own self-selected direction. As an article in the Shanghai-based *Shehui Kexue* suggests, the municipality suffered from a conspicuous case of investment hunger *(touzi ji'e zheng)*, and had been the object of flagrant neglect by the central government for a number of years.[18]

The vague character of the electronics guidelines put forth during the period from 1979–1981 derived from several factors. The most important was that a clear vision of Shanghai's vanguard role in China's modernization drive had not yet developed at the national level. Nor did a clear conception of how to combine regional and sectoral policies exist at that time. A 1982 article in the Shanghai journal *Social Sciences* complained that although China had imported seven production lines for the manufacturing of LSI in recent years and although Shanghai had very favorable—probably the best—conditions to produce such components, not one of these production lines had been installed in Shanghai.[19] The decision to bypass Shanghai reflected not merely the regional rivalry between the center and the localities in China, but also the general tendency (historical and contemporary) of the MEI to give preference to its own units over those belonging to the various municipal or provincial entities.

Within Shanghai's local government and academic circles as well, the issue of electronics development strategy also sparked a lively discussion. As early as 1979, a general debate on the municipality's economic strategy began. The debate centered on the advantages and weaknesses of Shanghai's industrial and economic system.[20] The main impetus for the debate was captured in an article in *Liaowang* written a few years later:

> Shanghai, this eye-catching old industrial base for the millions, is facing sharper and sharper challenges and the situation is becoming grimmer. . . . first, the fast rising revolution of the world's new technology has a direct impact on Shanghai, the commercial city of strategic importance on the Western shore of the Pacific. Second, the vigorous and rapid rise of the economies in fraternal provinces and cities at home since the Party's 3rd Plenum, Shanghai's losing of certain traditional advantages and its encountering of a number of strong opponents in competition have made Shanghai's 'leading position' more unstable. Third, the day when Shanghai could rely on cheap energy and raw materials and develop processing industries have gone forever and the contradictions caused by short supply of energy and raw materials are sharpening with each passing day.[21]

The main positions that comprised the elements of the debate dealt with means rather than ends.[22] Some argued that Shanghai's way out of its economic problems required additional emphasis on light industries and textiles. Others stressed that Shanghai should concentrate on transforming itself into a center for foreign trade. The majority of the discussants agreed, however, that priority should be given to the manufacture of new high-quality, highly sophisticated, and high-precision products. Because of Shanghai's technological level and management experiences, it was felt that these factors would facilitate the acquisition and absorption of foreign technology and thus support a move into high technology. The implications of this move toward high-tech industries were probably not fully recognized, since foreign experiences had been studied only to a limited extent. Nonetheless, many individuals believed that the arguments brought forward paved the way for a new industrial policy in Shanghai.[23]

The debate helped to clarify the specific role of the electronics industry within Shanghai's economic structure. This was quite important because of the aforementioned steel versus electronics debate that had existed since the 1960s. People saw the main advantages of the electronics industry as: it conserves raw materials and energy, the level of pollution is low, and the industry requires limited space for production. Moreover, electronics technology is both knowledge- and skill-intensive. Thus, a focus on the creation of an advanced electronics industry was regarded as a means to help Shanghai overcome some of its basic economic and social problems and establish the basis for a strategic shift in its economic underpinning.

Shanghai's development guidelines were reformulated after 1982, when changes in the principal thrust of China's overall economic development were announced at the Twelfth Party Congress and in the central government's program for the electronics industry. In particular, the announcement of the "quadrupling goal" for the entire economy, combined with the added emphasis placed on the role of science and technology, economic reforms, and a new regional policy, cast industrial centers such as Shanghai in a new light.[24] These changes resulted in a reassessment of Shanghai's role in the Chinese economy at the central level. In August 1983, Party Secretary Hu Yaobang visited Shanghai and pointed out that "Shanghai should play a vanguard role" in the country's four modernizations drive.[25] This visit also provided the impetus for the central government to look at Shanghai's economic future in a broader perspective.

The central leadership's growing awareness of the need to link sectoral and regional policies more closely was the general background for the changing attitude towards Shanghai. On the one hand, Beijing started to view the role of electronics as a possible pioneer industry in China's overall economic development. On the other hand, it was also recognized that the best way to solve the various economic and technological problems inhibiting the firm establishment of this pioneer role would be to focus development on a few select, advanced areas, such as Beijing and Shanghai.[26]

The reformulation of Shanghai's economic, industrial, and technological strategy, combined with the decision to create the Shanghai Economic Zone in December 1982, have their origins in this new regionally oriented development policy.[27] The zone's principal objectives were to enhance economic cooperation and integration between Shanghai and the adjacent provinces and to foster greater specialization and rationalization in production. Hence, the main driving force underlying Shanghai's development shifted back to the central government. Unlike the situation from 1978 to 1980, Beijing was more sensitive to Shanghai's identity as an independent economic center and to its unique problems. Officials in Shanghai were not necessarily completely pleased to be ostensibly taken under the wing of Beijing, since it appeared to local cadre that the new nurturing from Beijing might turn out to be another form of intervention by the central government in the city's affairs. Nonetheless, in spite of the rivalry between the two, the imperatives of overcoming Shanghai's complex problems helped forge an alliance of convenience.

The central authorities adopted several main steps to bring about this shift. After Hu Yaobang's visit to Shanghai in late summer 1983, the central leadership in Beijing began a systematic assessment of Shanghai's major industrial and technological strengths and weaknesses.[28] For this purpose, the State Council sent a high-level delegation to Shanghai to help the municipal authorities appraise the city's development strategy and work out an outline for future economic development. In the summer of 1984, the central authorities issued a number of public statements regarding Shanghai's role in the Chinese economy. At a seminar on the development strategy for Shanghai's economy in September 1984, Wang Daohan, then Mayor of Shanghai, summarized the attitude of the central government in Beijing as follows:

> In July [1984], Premier Zhao Ziyang made an important speech on 'creating conditions for transforming and revitalizing old bases' . . . Afterward, the party central leadership and the State Council issued many important instructions on Shanghai's economic work, requiring that Shanghai bring its role as a key port city into full play and that it function as a major economic, technological and cultural base in our country . . . Not only should Shanghai act as a major industrial base of our country, but should also act as China's largest economic center, providing better trade, financial, information, and technological services for economic construction throughout the country. [Therefore] Shanghai must make active efforts to apply new technology to the transformation of its traditional industries and to develop new industries while strengthening its infrastructural construction in order to vigorously develop the third industry.[29]

In December 1984, Premier Zhao Ziyang, accompanied by several high-ranking cadres, made an official inspection tour of Shanghai and received briefings about, among other things, the city's electronics industry.[30] Zhao's visit underscored the growing concerns in Beijing that China's leading industrial base, i.e. Shanghai, was not moving ahead as rapidly as desired in both its overall modernization and economic reforms.[31] In January 1985, the State Council formally approved the report on the "Strategies for Shanghai's Economic Development."[32] The report not only provided new guidelines for Shanghai's development, e.g. "industry is to abandon its reliance on cheap, quality products in favor of high technology-intensive quality consumer goods," but it also emphasized the need for Shanghai to become a major source of export earnings for the Chinese economy.[33]

As to Shanghai's electronics industry and its role within the city's industrial restructuring program, the central government in Beijing and the Shanghai municipal government initiated a number of specific measures. For example, to help transform Shanghai into a "high-tech center," the municipal S&T commission announced the "program for technological breakthroughs of large-scale integrated circuits in Shanghai, 1983–85."[34] Within this context, several key institutions (e.g. the Institute of Metallurgy of the Shanghai branch of the CAS, Fudan University, Shanghai Components Factory No. 5, and Shanghai Radio Factory No. 14) formed a microelectronics group to carry out joint LSI research and development. In order to create a more responsive and reliable components and computer industry, greater attention was paid to technical transformation projects in a number of key institutions. The State Economic Commission, for example, selected 148 electronics institutions from around the country to receive funds for plant renovation and rehabilitation. Even though only 20 of the 148 projects were in Shanghai, one-fourth of the 28 LSI and computer institutions were in Shanghai.[35] A critical change in perspective was taking place in Beijing. As one *Renmin Ribao* editorial on the ways to stimulate electronics development suggested:

> . . . it is necessary to take the whole country into account, bring into play the initiatives of the central authorities and the localities, work out good plans for enterprises, trades, and regions, *and* promote the combination and coordination of enterprises, trades and regions. In producing complete products and carrying out joint management, it is necessary to break the bonds of different regions, enterprises, and trades.[36]

The Shanghai Academy of Social Sciences (SASS) conducted an assessment of the potential impact of new technologies, and electronics in particular, on Shanghai's future industrial structure and economic performance. In the assessment, SASS worked out three scenarios which calculated the possible effects on gross production value and profits. The first scenario assumed that electronics would be Shanghai's core sector; the second, the traditional industries (metallurgy, chemical industry, machine-building, textile industry); the third, light and textile industries.[37] SASS concluded that Shanghai's economy would make the most substantial and rapid degree of progress if electronics were its core industry.[38] It was therefore decided to increase the share of the electronics industry (as well as that of other new technologies, like bioengineering, new materials, laser technology, fiber communications, and industrial robots) in Shanghai's agricultural and industrial gross production value.[39] Apart from an increase in the production of electronic products, emphasis was placed on the expanded application of electronic technology in order to improve the performance of so-called traditional industries.[40]

Electronics industry officials also envisaged a restructuring of the product mix. The main target was the computer industry; in 1984 the Shanghai Computer Corporation was moved out from under the control of the Instrumentation and Electronics Bureau and placed under the direct jurisdiction of the Shanghai Economic Commission.[41] Shanghai's share of gross production value of computers to be increased, the focus of production was to be shifted to mini- and microcomputers.[42] This shift was accompanied by a projected restructuring in the research and production of semiconductor components. LSIs were then being produced only in small quantities; future efforts would focus on mass production of LSIs. In Shanghai's Caohejing district the construction of an LSI research and production base to manufacture advanced components was also begun.

According to the new guidelines, highest attention would be paid to the quality and reliability of Shanghai's electronic products. In a survey conducted by a group from the former State Machine Building Commission of the Shanghai electronics and machine-building industry, the reasons for the "backward nature" of local products in the past were highlighted:

> An important reason for the low quality of our mechanical and electrical products is that our basic mechanical products and electronic components are poor in quality. Another reason is that the quality of our basic machinery is low. We have a large quantity of machinery, but it is characterized by low quality, low precision, low speed, and high noise level. In particular, we lack some key precision machine tools, such as digital-controlled machine tools, and consequently we cannot produce high precision parts. We also do not have enough precision measuring and testing apparatuses to check the quality of processing . . . with low quality basic machinery we are still able to produce some quality products, but we cannot mass produce them, and this is our weakest point.[43]

The move towards better quality was designed to improve the competitiveness of goods originating from the municipality in the domestic market, but it was also a necessary step for Shanghai to gain a foothold in world markets.

These initiatives and discussions from 1982 to 1984 set the stage for a new strategic approach to Shanghai's overall industrial development. More specifically, industries such as electronics were given a higher priority in the modernization drive—both at the national level and the local level. In January 1984, Shanghai's Deputy Mayor, Liu Zhenyuan, a former senior researcher in CAS's Shanghai-based Institute of Metallurgy who was responsible for overseeing electronics development, announced that electronics had been classified as a "first priority industry."[44] The notion of creating Silicon Valley equivalents in Shanghai and several other parts of China also emerged. All of these innovations in approach were designed to break through the political obstacles and economic barriers that had been formed in Shanghai over the past three decades. One culmination of these efforts was the decision in mid-1985 to replace Wang Daohan as mayor and Chen Guodong as Party Secretary. Ironically, in his place, the central government appointed Jiang Zemin— who not only previously worked in Shanghai, but more significantly, was the former Minister of the Electronics Industry.

THE ORGANIZATIONAL STRUCTURE OF SHANGHAI'S ELECTRONICS INDUSTRY

Figure 4–2 shows the organization of Shanghai's electronics industry. Functional responsibility for its management belongs to the Bureau of Electronics and Instrumentation (*Dianzi Yibiao Ju*), hereafter referred to as the Bureau. The Bureau oversees the planning, research, and production associated with all facets of electronics. It also handles the marketing of products, although items such as color television sets are still sold through State distribution channels. Until reforms introduced in late 1986, eight corporations fell under the direct administrative management of the bureau: broadcasting and television; electronics components; vacuum devices; optical instruments; electronic instruments; testing instrumentation; semiconductors; and electronics import and export affairs (SEIECO). The Shanghai Computer Corporation was removed from the Bureau's control in 1984 and placed directly under the control of the municipal economic commission. This decision was

Figure 4–2. Shanghai's Electronics Industry (1986).

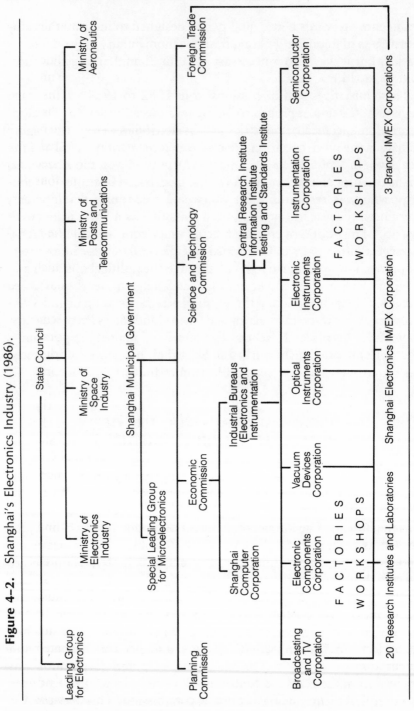

Source: Shanghai Bureau of Electronics and Instrumentation, 1986.

intended to give greater flexibility and visibility to computer development in the municipality.

Each corporation managed a number of manufacturing facilities; their work was supported jointly by approximately twenty research units and laboratories, six of which could be considered key research institutes. According to Chinese explanations, an industrial corporation "is a form of rational economic integration of scattered factories on the basis of specialization and coordination."[45] Excluding foreign invested enterprises, these corporations fall into two broad categories: specialized companies and local joint venture companies. There are basically four types of specialized corporations in Shanghai:

1. Specialized product companies, which manufacture one type of product, e.g. Shanghai Computer Corporation
2. Specialized technological processing corporations, which concentrate on one specific production process, e.g. Shanghai Cotton Textile Manufacturing Corporation
3. Specialized components corporations, which produce specific parts and components, e.g. Shanghai Semiconductor Corporation
4. Specialized industrial service corporations, which distribute industrial-type services, e.g. Shanghai Packaging Corporation.[46]

There are two types of local joint venture companies. First, there are joint production corporations. The majority of these are in the chemical industry, e.g. the Gaoqiao Petrochemical Corporation, the Shanghai Petrochemical Corporation, and the Wujin Joint Chemical Corporation. Second are what the Chinese term "joint production and marketing" companies. These are relatively few in number, involving mainly facilities in such industries as toys.

These corporations have been important since their founding in the 1950s. In recent years, however, many questions have been raised about their economic performance and efficiency (See Chapter 6). In this structure, a factory sits under the leadership of a corporation or company which is usually subordinate to a bureau. The bureaus are led by the municipal government through various commissions. To make decisions regarding changes in planning, production, finances, technical renovation, and sales, factories must go through a complicated maze of bureaucracy, beginning with the corporation and sometimes ending up in Beijing.[47] The corporations often have evolved into no more than administrative organizations. The problem of *guanliao zhuyi*, or "bureaucratism," is frequently cited by Chinese officials as a key bottleneck in the modernization drive.

While the MEI does not supervise any production facilities in Shanghai, it does supervise several key research institutes. Many of these perform defense-related R&D; they include the East China Computer Research Institute (#32), the Shanghai Institute of Transmission Lines (#23), the Shanghai Institute of Microwave Technology, the Shanghai Institute of Microwave Equipment, and the Shanghai Micromotors Research Institute. The production units of other ministries, however, are strongly represented within the boundaries of the municipality. The term "systems–within–a–system" refers to the presence of these other ministerial entities located in Shanghai but generally outside the administrative control of the Shanghai government.

The extent of bureaucratic compartmentalization tends to be a function of the amount of military-related activities carried out by these units. For example, the Ministry of Space Industry (MSI) has a number of key electronics production facilities in Shanghai.[48] Many of these facilities are under the umbrella of the Shanghai Bureau of Astronautics (Hangtian Ju), the former #2 Electrical Machinery Bureau, which is run directly by the MSI. Heretofore, these various units have had little if any direct role in Shanghai's overall economic and technology planning.[49] The National Defense Science, Technology, and Industry Commission (NDSTIC) does have an office in Shanghai. This office is tasked with coordinating the various ministerial and local units that may be involved in any NDSTIC-sponsored military research or manufacturing activities.

Three commissions under the municipal government play a direct role in managing and funding Shanghai's electronics and computer industry: the Science and Technology Commission, the Planning Commission, and the Economic Commission. Responsibilities are divided between the R&D side and production side of the industry; this often creates coordination problems. The local science and technology commission (STC) oversees research activities related to electronics by setting local priorities and serving as a conduit for central government projects sponsored by the State Science and Technology Commission in Beijing. Through the Department of Integrated Planning under the STC, specific guidelines and targets are provided for various scientific and technical fields. The STC works closely with the local planning commission to ensure that necessary funds are made available to carry out proposed projects.

The main function of the Planning Commission is to translate central directives into specific long-term and short-term targets for the Shanghai municipality. It also is responsible for managing and supporting capital construction projects in the city. The Planning Commission receives project proposals and plans from each industrial bureau and related entities; these are actually requests for funding from the various departments under the local government. The commission must sort out the competing funding requests and ensure that the plans of all participating bureaus are well coordinated. The primary responsibility for the day-to-day, on-the-ground activities in the industrial sector belongs to the Economic Commission. This commission focuses most of its attention on manufacturing, product quality and standards, etc. Its most important duty is to handle all monies in the budget associated with the program on the technical transformation of enterprises—which in Shanghai is considered to be a key element in the ongoing effort to improve productivity and economic efficiency.

The Bureau reports directly to the municipal Economic Commission, which along with the other two commissions, develops two types of plans: (1) a broad framework for electronics *(guihua)* which identifies the general orientation and defines the focus of the industry over a period of several years, e.g. the extent to which consumer versus military electronics will be emphasized and (2) the concrete plan *(jihua)* which contains the specific targets and goals that must be met. These two types of plans are supplemented by projects that are sponsored and financed from above by the central government, which could include various ministries, commissions, and the CAS.

The most important recent structural development has been the creation in summer 1983 of a municipal-level special leading group for electronics that reports directly to the Mayor's office.[50] The special leading group, also known as the *Da Ban,* meaning "LSI office," was created to provide some coherence to Shanghai's efforts to create a base for high technology industries such as microelectronics. Unlike Beijing municipality's, Shanghai's leading group has no official representation or direct ties to the national leading group for electronics other than through that group's advisory mechanisms. This is somewhat strange in view of the fact that several of China's most advanced microelectronics facilities—#5 Components Factory, #7 Radio Factory, #14 Radio Factory and #19 Radio Factory—are located in Shanghai.[51]

Shanghai's decision to set up this leading group was very much in keeping with the thinking underlying the State Council's decision to establish a similar body. In fact, both groups were set up to focus on computers and LSI but eventually decided that other areas such as telecommunications should be included in their responsibilities. Yet, while the role of the State Council leading group in the overall development of China's electronics industry has become increasingly clear, knowledge about the precise role of the Shanghai leading group is still limited. In principle, Shanghai's leading group must follow the spirit of the plans and priorities set by the State Council electronics leading group—thus focusing on microelectronics, computers, and communications. However, its lack of direct ties to the State Council group may allow it some divergence of focus, in line with the municipality's own goals, which are largely a product of its historical relationship with Beijing. The major constraint on its ability to take independent actions is its dependence on Beijing for the bulk of its funding.

Research activities in Shanghai's electronics industry are carried out by three major groups (see Figure 4–3). The first consists of over forty institutes managed by central government ministries and commissions, including the CAS.[52] These institutes tend to be fairly large, with an average staff of about 560 persons, and generally are well-equipped compared with their local counterparts. The second group is institutes under the universities, which total almost fifty. Even though they tend to address fairly new research topics, such as artificial intelligence, these institutes are generally small, with an average staff of twenty-four persons. Some of the key institutions include Fudan University, Shanghai Jiaotong University, and Shanghai S&T University. The third group consists of twenty-three institutes under municipal control, both within and outside of the Bureau. Most of these entities are oriented toward meeting the needs of their functional branches (hangye). Researchers and staff in this group totalled more than 4200 persons at the beginning of 1985, of which 1790, or 42 percent, were S&T personnel. (See Table 4–1.)

A major part of electronics research and development in Shanghai is performed by the Shanghai branch of the CAS. Out of the fifteen research units it supervises in Shanghai, four have particular relevance to electronics: Institute of Metallurgy (IoM), Institute of Ceramics, Institute of Technical Physics, and Institute of Optics and Fine Mechanics. The IoM was founded in 1928 along with the Institute of Ceramics and was made an independent unit in 1959.[53] At present, the IoM is engaged in three major research areas: microelectronics, special materials, and corrosion and protection of metals. The research work in electronics focuses on LSI technologies, superconducting materials,

Figure 4-3. Shanghai's Electronics R&D System.

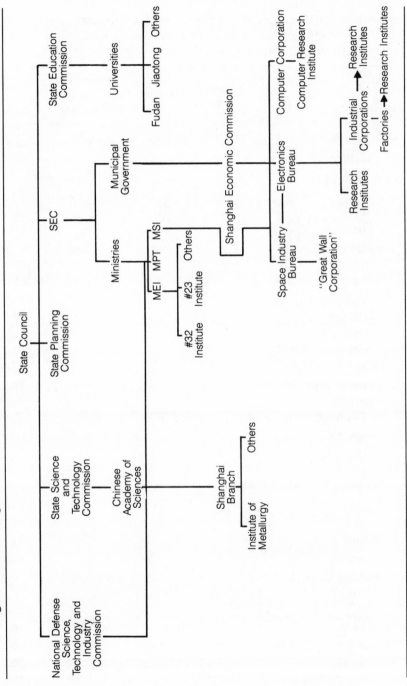

Source: Shanghai Electronics and Instrumentation Bureau, Shanghai, 1985.

Table 4-1. Number of Employees and Engineers, and Technicians in Selected Institutions of Shanghai's Electronics Industry.

Enterprise/Institute	Number of Employees	Number of Engineers and Technicians	Percentage
A. Bureau of Instrumentation Electronics	160,000	16,000	10
B. IC producers:			
Components Factory #5	1,580	300	18.9
Radio Factory #7	2,000	300	15
Radio Factory #14	1,156	346	30
Radio Factory #19	1,200	200	16.6
C. Computer producers:			
Shanghai Computer Corporation	4,500	1,000	22.2
D. Local Semiconductor Research Institutes:			
Vacuum Tube Research Institute	300	100	33.3
Semiconductor Research Institute	780	210	27
E. Shanghai Branch, CAS			
Institute of Metallurgy (CAS)	1,250	750	60
F. Ministry of Electronics:			
East China Institute of Computer Technology	1,241	682	54.9
G. Ministry of Space Industry:			
Electronic Communications Equipment Research Institute	550	300	54.5
Shanghai Radio Equipment Institute	500	257	51.4

Sources: Interviews conducted in Shanghai, July 1985.

magnetic materials and devices, new processes and technologies for integrated devices, and gallium arsenide technology. Along with the Institute of Semiconductors under the CAS in Beijing, these two institutes compete for the leading position (and related funding) as China's premier IC R&D facility.[54]

At times, the IoM is placed in a rather awkward position, both having local ties and receiving its support from the central administration of the CAS in Beijing. Although it continues to experience difficulties producing "relevant" research results, it has also been extremely successful at building a workable set of both horizontal and vertical ties to support its research activities.[55] These links helped provide the impetus for the realization of forty-five scientific and technological achievements, the most in the history of the institute. More important, perhaps, these achievements brought more than 10 million yuan in revenue.

Although the plethora of different systems engaged in the research and application of electronics technology has led to the emergence of distinct vertical barriers between the various units, a number of cross-organizational linkages have developed. For example, the East China Research Institute of Computer Technology under the MEI, one of China's most advanced institutes in the computer industry, has established over more than twenty years' worth of close relations with several of Shanghai's leading manufacturing units, including the Shanghai Computer Factory. Similarly, most other institutes run by the MEI and the CAS in Shanghai, are also integrated, through a number of joint projects, into Shanghai's local electronics research system.[56]

To facilitate such horizontal linkages between these centrally controlled units and local institutions and to coordinate research activities, the Shanghai Academy of Sciences (SAS) was founded in November 1977. The SAS is separate from the Shanghai branch of the CAS, though ironically they share many of the same leading personnel.[57] Its main function is to provide support services, guidance, and material assistance to those facilities belonging to the central government. In many respects, its existence shows the discrepancy between central and local perspectives regarding the control and management of organizations within and outside their direct administrative jurisdictions. With respect to electronics, the SAS supervises four out of five of the MEI's institutes in Shanghai—the Shanghai Micromotor Institute, the Shanghai Institute for Transmission Lines, the East China Computer Research Institute, and the Shanghai Institute for Microwave Technology. For the most part, the resources to keep these entities running do not come from Shanghai's coffers; the SAS appears to procure the necessary resources from Shanghai for a fee.

NOTES

1. Municipal Statistical Bureau of Shanghai, *Economic and Social Development in Shanghai, 1985* (Shanghai, 1986). State Statistical Bureau, ed., *Statistical Yearbook of China 1986* (Beijing: China Statistics Publishing House, 1986). *Wenhui Bao*, March 6, 1987. *Renmin Ribao*, February 21, 1987.

2. Feng Zhijun, "Research on Shanghai's Strategic Countermeasures for the New Technological Revolution." *Shijie Jingji Wenhui* (World Economy Forum), no. 4 (October/December 1984): 32–38, translated in *Joint Publications Research Service—China Economic Affairs 85-031*, March 25, 1985, pp. 72–84.

3. Xu Fulan, "Shanghai gongye shengchan zenyang zou neihan kuodao zai shengchan daolu" (The manner in which Shanghai's industrial production should take the road to 'intensive' reproduction on an extended scale), *Shehui Kexue* (Social Sciences), no. 6 (1983): 5–6. See also "Shanghai Faces Talent Shortage," *China Daily*, November 24, 1984.

4. Xu Fulan, "The Manner."

5. "Why Is Shanghai's Development of New Products So Sluggish." *Shijie Jingji Daobao* (World Economic Herald), February 28, 1983, p. 10 translated in *Joint Publications Research Service 83413*, May 5, 1983, pp. 11–13.

6. According to one source, as of mid-1984, electronics and other newly developed industries constituted a mere 4.4 percent of overall industrial composition, while traditional industries made up more than 90 percent. Moreover, labor-intensive industry constituted 49 percent, capital-intensive industry 34 percent, and technology-intensive industry a mere 17 percent of the industrial sector. See Luo Hoxiang and Zhu Xiangxian, "Meet the Challenge and Realize the Strategic Readjustment of Shanghia's Industry," *Caijing Yanjiu*, no. 3 (June 25, 1984): 1–5, translated in *Joint Publications Research Service—China Economic Affairs 84-099*, December 6, 1984, pp. 50–59.

7. Economic Research Institute, Shanghai Academy of Social Sciences, ed., *Shanghai Minzu Jiqi Gongye* (Shanghai's national machine-building industry), 2 vols. (Beijing: Zhonghua Shuju Publishing, 1979).

8. Today, this factory is under the administrative jurisdiction of the Ministry of Space Industry. It is managed by the Great Wall Industry Corporation, which is under the control of the space industry bureau, formerly known as the Shanghai #2 Electrical Machinery Bureau.

9. Among the institutes which were set up in 1958 are the Institute for Technical Physics (Jishu Wuli Yanjiusuo) under the Chinese Academy of Sciences which focuses on semiconductor physics and technologies, and the East China Institute of Computer Technology which developed one of China's first computers.

10. Discussions in Shanghai, July 1985.

11. N. Lardy, *Economic Growth and Distribution in China* (Cambridge: Cambridge University Press, 1978).

12. Between 1956 and 1980, central investment in capital construction of Shanghai's electronics and instrumentation industry accounted for only 2.8 percent of the branch profits which were remitted to the central budget in the same period. See Chen Minzhi and Huang Zhenyu, "Cong Shanghai gongye fazhan tan tan zou neihan xing kuoda zai shengchan de luzi" (Against the background of Shanghai's industrial development to an intense-type path of enlarged reproduction," *Jingji Yanjiu* (Economic Research), no. 6 (1982): 22–27.

13. "Shanghai dianzi gongye cong wu dao you xian xing rong" (The glorious development of Shanghai's electronics industry from scratch), *Wenhui Bao,* September 19, 1979.

14. For example, in a similar way the electonics industry in Changzhou was established. See Detlef Rehn, *The Electronics Age Comes to China— The Case of Changzhou City (Jiangsu Province)* (Bonn: Ostasien-Insitut, 1984), especially pp. 49–52.

15. Discussions in Shanghai, July 1985.

16. "Develop vigorously computers in an independent and self-reliant manner," *Ziran Bianzhengfa* (Dialectics of Nature), No. 4 (1974), pp. 46–56. According to a report of 1979, there were 205 computers in use in Shanghai. However, only one-fifth to one-fourth were described as being well-used. "Rang jisuanji wu jin qi yong" (Allow computers to be used in the best way), *Wenhui Bao,* May 17, 1979.

17. The reason for the near collapse was that the inflexibility that came from dependence on a structure that relied heavily upon large and medium systems. This prevented a quick shift to the production of microcomputers, which were seen as more appropriate for China's overall needs. Thus, it turned out that other provinces with a less developed computer industry had a substantial advantage over Shanghai. Accordingly, the gross production value of Shanghai's computer industry, which in 1979 amounted to RMB 100m, dropped by 26 percent in 1980, and by another 56 percent in 1981. "How to open a way for computers made in Shanghai," *Shijie Jingji Daobao* (World Economic Herald), October 18, 1982.

18. Yu Riqing, "Take a Further Step in Fostering the Regulatory Effects of Taxes," *Shehui Kexue,* no. 8 (August 1983): 25–29.

19. Xu Zhihe and Li Douhan: "A Preliminary Survey of the Rationalization of Shanghai's Industrial Structure," *Shehui Kexue* (Social Sciences), no. 1 (1982): 25–29.

20. *Shanghai Jingji Fazhan Zhanlue Wenji* (Selections on Shanghai's Economic Development Strategy) (Shanghai: Shanghai Academy of Social Sciences, 1984).

21. Shen Shiwei, "A Brand New Strategic Target—Experts, Scholars and People in Economic Circles Discuss Countermeasures for Shanghai's Economic Development," *Liaowang*, no. 44, (October 29, 1984): 22–23, translated in *Joint Publications Research Service—China Economic Affairs 85-021*, February 28, 1985, pp. 35–38.

22. For an overview of the different issues under discussion at that time see Shen Junbo et al., "Guanyu Shanghai changyuan guihua de ge zhong jianjie" (Views regarding Shanghai's Long-term Program), *Shehui Kexue*, no. 3 (1981): 70–75.

23. Chen Minzhi, ed., *Shanghai Jingji Fazhan Zhanlue Yanjiu* (Research on Shanghai's Economic Development Strategy) (Shanghai: People's Publishing House, 1985).

24. Wang Daohan, "Report on Several Major Works in the Course of the Current Economic and Social Development of Shanghai," *Jiefang Ribao* (Liberation Daily), December 31, 1982, p. 2, translated in *Joint Publications Research Service 82963*, February 28, 1983, pp. 1–24.

25. "Shanghai Will Be Built Into the Largest Economic Center of the Country," *Zhongguo Xinwen She*, March 17, 1985, translated in *Foreign Broadcast Information Service—People's Republic of China*, March 19, 1985, p. K20.

26. At the aforementioned "Third National Conference for the Development of large-scale integrated circuits" in late 1982, Zhao Dongwan, then vice-minister of the State Scientific and Technological Commission revealed the plan of the central government to establish two industrial bases for LSI research and production in the Beijing-Tianjin-Shenyang area and in the Shanghai-Jiangsu-Zhejiang area. See *Xinhua News Agency* (in English), December 23, 1982.

27. See, for example, Zhou Taihe, ed., *Dangdai Zhongguo Jingji Tizhi Gaige* (Reforms of the Economic System in Present China), part 3, ch. 1: "Reforms of Shanghai's economic system," (Beijing: China Social Sciences Publishing House, 1984), pp. 527–580.

28. "Liaowang Presents Shanghai as Economic Center," *Foreign Broadcast Information Service China*, March 19, 1985, pp. K20–21.

29. "Central Leaders Point the Way Forward for Revitalizing Shanghai," *Jingji Ribao* (Economic Daily), September 24, 1984, translated in *Joint Publications Research Service—China Economic Affairs 84-087*, pp. 2–3.

30. Jin Dongmin, "Shanghai Should Promote Its Role as National Economic Center," *Wenhui Bao* (Wenhui Daily), January 16, 1985, p. 1, translated in *Joint Publications Research Service—China Economic Affairs 85-040*, pp. 1–5.

31. One area where reforms had not proceeded ahead was price reform. According to one report from the SASS, "When controls for extra plan means of production were relaxed in most provinces and municipalities throughout the country, Shanghai persisted in inflexible price control measures. . . . When restrictive controls for agriculture and sideline products . . . were relaxed and replaced by trade at negotiated prices in many provinces and municipalities, Shanghai persisted in not relaxing, or in slightly relaxing such controls. . . . When the state had prescribed that pricing of small commodities of the third category should be relegated to the enterprises and prices be negotiated between industry and commerce, Shanghai was slow in taking action and did not promptly implement the prescribed measures." See Li Fan and Zhang Hongming, "Shanghai de jiage gaige" (Price Reform in Shanghai), *Shanghai Jingji*, no. 2, (April 15, 1985): 9–11.

32. "Shanghai's Economic Strategy is Geared Toward the Pacific," *Ta Kung Pao*, May 12, 1985, p. 3, translated in *Foreign Broadcast Information Service—People's Republic of China*, May 16, 1985, pp. W1–3.

33. "State Council Approves Shanghai Development Plan," *Xinhua*, March 14, 1985, translated in *Foreign Broadcast Information Service—People's Republic of China*, March 15, 1985, p. K28.

34. "Da guimo jicheng dianlu huizhan si lu gaojie" (Victories in the LSI battle along four ways), *Wenhui Bao* (Wenhui Daily), July 8, 1983.

35. *Jixie Zhoubao* (Machine Building Weekly), no. 149 (July 29, 1983): 2.

36. "Actively Develop the Electronics Industry in a Well Coordinated Manner," *Renmin Ribao*, March 2, 1984, p. 1.

37. Yao Xitang et al., "The New Technological Revolution and the Readjustment of Shanghai's Economic Structure," in *Shanghai Jingji Fazhan Zhanlüe Wenti*, pp. 49–71.

38. Ibid. The decision to treat electronics as a core sector by Shanghai officials meant that it would be targeted to receive additional funds and resources so that by 1990 its share of Shanghai's gross value of industrial output (GVIO) would be 6.76 percent (up from 4.6 percent in 1980) and in the year 2000 it would be 13.33 percent—and thus it would be Shanghai's largest industrial sector.

39. Ibid., pp. 62–63. By re-focusing investment and resource allocation, Shanghai officials hoped to readjust the ratio of labor, capital and technology intensive industry from 49:34:17 in 1980 to 35:26:39 in the year 2000.

40. Chen Minzhi and Yao Xitang, "Goal options in Shanghai's economic development strategy," in Chen Minzhi, ed., *Shanghai Jingji Fazhan Zhanlüe Yanjiu,* (Investigation on Shanghai's economic development strategy) (Shanghai, People's Publishing House, 1985), pp. 6–22.

41. See Liu Zhenyuan, "Shattering the Fetters of Old Ideology and Blazing a New Trail in Making Reforms," *Renmin Ribao,* June 29, 1984, p. 2.

42. The recent decision of the "State Council Leading Group for the Revitalization of the Electronics Industry" to select Beijing as China's main production site for large and medium-sized computer systems will support this shift. See *Zhongguo Dianzi Bao,* October 22, 1985.

43. Zong Tang, "The Reorganization, Reform, and Revitalization of China's Machine-Building Industry as Seen from Shanghai," *Hongqi,* no. 3, (February 1, 1982): 24–28, translated in *Joint Publications Research Service 80469,* April 1, 1982, pp. 41–49.

44. *China Daily,* January 5, 1984, p. 2.

45. Dong Ronglin, "Give Play to the Role of Industrial Corporations in Promoting Technical Progress," *Renmin Ribao,* April 23, 1984, p. 5.

46. Gong Xuelin and Chen Jiaqiu, "Shanghai gongye qiye zuzhi jiegou helihua de yanjiu" (Study of the Rationalization of the Organizational Structure of Shanghai's Industrial Enterprises), *Shehui Kexue,* no. 5 (May 15, 1983): 28–31.

47. "Companies to Disband in Shanghai," *China Daily,* August 1, 1986.

48. Among these facilities are the Shanghai Broadcasting Equipment Factory, the Shanghai Precision Machinery Corporation, the Shanghai Wire Communications Factory, the Great Wall Industrial Corporation, the Shanghai Xin Li Machinery Factory, and the Shanghai Scientific Instruments Factory.

49. These facilities receive their tasking primarily from the MSI or the NDSTIC due to their military-oriented character. The extent of overall compartmentation, however, has begun to change with the emphasis being placed on military-to-civilian technology transfer since 1984.

50. Prior to summer 1986, Deputy Mayor Liu Zhenyuan had functional responsibility for managing the leading group for electronics. With the arrival of former MEI Minister Jiang Zemin as mayor of Shanghai, that responsibility seems to have been placed directly in Jiang's hands. As of 1988, it seems to have shifted back into Liu's portfolio.

51. The Beijing Municipal leading group for electronics also has representatives from the Ministry of Electronics Industry, the State Science and Technology Commission, the CAS, the State Education Commission, and the National Defense Science, Technology and Industries Commission as well as members from the municipal government. See *Beijing Ribao* October 18, 1985, p. 1.

52. A good example is provided by the MSI, which has a number of key research institutes in Shanghai. These include Shanghai Radio Equipment Institute, Shanghai Institute for Precision Devices, Shanghai Institute for Electronic Communications Equipment, Shanghai Institute for Precision Measuring and Testing, and the Shanghai Satellite Engineering Institute.

53. The IoM has given birth to three independent research institutes in the past: Changsha Institute of Mining and Metallurgy, the Kunming Institute of Noble Metals, and the Shanghai Institute of Ceramics.

54. Based on discussions in Shanghai and Beijing, it is not too uncommon to find these two institutes competing with each other for funds and support regarding various semiconductor/IC projects. For example, during the summer 1985, both were vying to obtain central government support for a 3-micron LSI project as well as an IC project dealing with the use of gallium arsenide.

55. "Shanghai Institute Director Impact on Reforms Discussed," *Renmin Ribao* (overseas ed.), November 28, 1986, p. 4.

56. "Metallurgy Institute Gears Up for S&T Development," *Jiefang Ribao*, November 8, 1985, p. 1, translated in *Joint Publications Research Service—China Science and Technology 86-010*, March 19, 1986, pp. 23–24.

57. See *Shanghai Keji, 1949–1984*, pp. 30–33.

5 INNOVATION IN SHANGHAI'S ELECTRONICS INDUSTRY
The Case of the Semiconductor Components Industry

The semiconductor industry is one of the most important industrial sectors in modern economies. Advances in semiconductor performance and capabilities have affected the pace and extent of technological change in the electronics industry by influencing the development of new generations of computers, advanced telecommunications equipment, new types of consumer electronics goods, etc. Technological advances in the semiconductor industry have also paved the way for the gradual diffusion of electronics into all sectors of the economy and society, thus laying the foundation for the information revolution.

During the last several years, the speed of technological change in the semiconductor industry has considerably increased. The era of the very large-scale integrated circuits (VLSI) started in 1979 when the 64K dynamic random access memory (DRAM) was developed. By 1983, successful development of a 256K DRAM was announced: mass production and sales started in 1984. In 1985, the technology for a 1-megabit chip was introduced. Even though marketing of this device has only just begun, attention already has begun to focus on the introduction of a far more sophisticated chip, the 4-megabit chip—which in all likelihood will be developed and actively marketed by the end of this decade.

Underlying this rapid pace of innovation are a number of critical factors.[1] First, after the initial research has been completed, an enormous amount of capital investment is required to build new facilities and install new equipment to adopt new process technologies. The overall cost of setting up a state-of-the-art, highly automated facility has continued to grow. For example, while in the late 1960s a capital investment of $500,000 was needed to remain successful in the semiconductor industry, the minimum investment required has increased to more than $10 million in the early 1980s.[2]

Second, because production has been routinized and production-related economies of scale have made themselves felt, the prices of the chips have been constantly declining—causing profits to drop for many of the major manufacturers, especially in the United States. For example, 64K RAMs were selling for $5 each in 1983; today, the price has gone down to $.60 or so due to the emergence of the 256K RAMs, overcapacities in production, and a declining demand worldwide. While sensitive to market share, manufacturers must also strive to be the first to introduce a new semiconductor component into the market in order to sustain a constant flow of profits.[3] Thus, the rapidity through which the product cycle for semiconductors runs its course serves to enhance the speed and commitment to innovation.[4]

The global semiconductor market is dominated by Japan and the United States, which together account for about 90 percent of the total production.[5] Western Europe is trailing far behind. In the mid-1980s, the worldwide semiconductor market, which had always been dominated by the United States, fell under the control of Japan. The Japanese now dominate 90 percent of the DRAM market, and more than 50 percent of the electrically programmable read-only memory (EPROM) market. They are making inroads in microprocessors, application-specific ICs, and static RAMs.[6] This does not mean that Japanese domination is a foregone conclusion. An interesting newcomer in the market is South Korea, which recently has undertaken massive efforts to establish its own VLSI industry, mainly by importing technology and forming various types of alliances with foreign—especially American—firms. Most recently, Taiwan also has announced a multi-billion dollar program to enter into VLSI production.

Stimulated by recent developments in the semiconductor industry abroad and by the continuing discussion of the nature and the concepts of industrial innovation in the West, the Chinese have begun to examine their approach to industrial innovation and, specifically, the conditions to enter the highly dynamic semiconductor market. As noted in Chapter 3, Chinese leaders consider technological progress in microelectronics to be one of their country's highest national priorities. As a result, leaders have been discussing how to speed up innovation and technological progress in the semiconductor industry ever since the formal inception of the modernization program in 1978.

The process of technological innovation usually includes "the technical, commercial and production steps necessary for the commercial production of a new product, or the first commercial use of a new process or equipment."[7] In China, commercialization of new products and processes heretofore has not been given serious attention.[8] This is an important reason why the technological gap between China and the industrialized countries in a number of key industrial sectors has continued to widen. Today, technical innovations and their diffusion are still widely characterized by the "three lows": low level of sophistication, low innovation speed, and low economic results from newly developed products.[9]

The semiconductor industry illustrates the various bottlenecks in the Chinese system which have inhibited rapid innovation. China's first integrated circuit was developed as early as 1964, representing a technological gap between China and the industrialized nations of only about five years. However, due to a variety of political factors as well as innovation-related problems, this gap has since considerably widened. According to various assessments by Western specialists, the actual level of China's IC R&D corresponds roughly to the international level of the late 1970s. More critical, production technology is even further behind. With some exceptions, integration densities of 1K and 4K are prevalent, and the line widths of most integrated circuits are no smaller than 5 to 6 microns—representing a gap of more than fifteen years compared with the current levels in the advanced industrialized countries.

In order to close these technological and economic gaps, China's electronics industry, in particular the semiconductor industry, has been undergoing a basic restructuring process. The primary elements of this process include a number of major organizational, technological, and economic reforms, such as the introduction of a contract system. These reforms aim to encourage market elements to play a more appreciable role in China's future S&T and innovation policy.

Shanghai has been assigned a major role in the process of reorganizing and restructuring China's semiconductor industry. This relates both to the effort to raise current technological levels and to the strides being made to establish a manufacturing base for LSI to help China become less dependent upon imports from abroad. Our analysis of the innovation process in Shanghai's semiconductor industry will focus on three major areas. These include the organization of Shanghai's components industry and the process of decision making, the incentives which are introduced into the Chinese system to improve weak innovation in the components sector, and the factors which influence the setting of objectives in China's electronics components industry.[10]

THE TECHNOLOGICAL LEVELS OF SHANGHAI'S SEMICONDUCTOR INDUSTRY

Innovation in Shanghai's components industry is carried out at different levels and in a number of ways. In China, the innovation process is formally split up into three distinct processes: scientific research; development, i.e. the activities to transform scientific results into new products and processes; and actual production, batch and serial.[11] The main actors engaged in innovation in Shanghai's components industry include the enterprises and research institutes under the local Bureau of Electronics and Instrumentation, the Institute of Metallurgy of the CAS's Shanghai branch, and universities such as Fudan University and Jiaotong University. The quantitative potential is considerable. Looking at the capabilities for research and development of ICs, for instance, Shanghai has a work force of over 1,000 semiconductor engineers and technicians—one-sixth of the national total.[12]

In the last few years, this potential has generated a number of important R&D results. One of the more recent achievements has been the development of an intelligent analysis and design system for ICs, the first of its kind in China, by the Institute of Automation and the Shanghai Institute of Metallurgy of the CAS. The system can automatically analyze large-scale circuits and redesign and verify layouts with the help of a computer.[13] A related achievement was the creation of a software package for VLSI design and testing by Shanghai Jiaotong University.[14] These results have received scientific and technical achievement awards in China—and they have also received attention at the international level. (See Table 5–1.)

A comparison of these *research* results—which at the time of their development probably represented the cutting edge of the technological level in Shanghai as well as most of China—with the *production* performances of the components sector reveals striking technological disparities. The Shanghai semiconductor industry has made substantial

Table 5-1.   Selected R&D Results in the Shanghai
Components Industry.

Unit	Product Specification	Year of Development
A. Products		
Institute of Metallurgy	4K SRAM (4 microns)	1985
	CMOS RAM (2 microns) 16K[a]	1985
Components Factory #5	4K DRAM	1983
	16K DRAM	1984
B. Process-related Results Radio Factory #14 + Fudan University Institute of Non-Ferrous Metals, Factory #740)	IC production line (MSI, SSI, Si wafer, 75 mm diameter)	1983
NA[a]	25 Hz graphic alpha-numeric generator	1985
Institute of Metallurgy	LSI CAD mask-making system	1985
Shanghai Jiaotong University	VLSI design & testing software system	1987

Sources: Personal communication, July 1985; *Zhongguo Baike Nianjian* (China's Yearbook), 1983–84; *Wenhui Bao* (Wenhui Daily), October 27, 1985; *WHB*, January 6, 1986; *Renmin Ribao* (People's Daily), December 31, 1983; *Zhongguo Dianzi Bao* (China Electronics), October 22, 1985.
    [a]Not confirmed.

progress in R&D during the last few years; many of Shanghai's leading R&D facilities possess up-to-date, advanced equipment to carry out their research activities. Most production, however, still widely relies on dated manufacturing technologies and a low level of automation. In 1985, for example, only 1 percent of total IC production in Shanghai was composed of LSIs, a level well below the national average of about 4 percent.[15] Thus, while the R&D sector has been able to push ahead, the manufacturing plants have not been able to easily or smoothly translate new research results into mass production.

The IC industry in Shanghai has been able to utilize existing equipment, some imported, and facilities towards meeting domestic demands for small and medium-scale integrated circuits. The Shanghai #14 Radio Factory produces two main products: field effect transistors (FETs) and CMOS integrated circuits. Among the seventeen factories that manufacture CMOS circuits in China, the majority of which are producing at the small-scale and medium-scale integration levels, the #14 Factory accounted for 52 percent of all CMOS output in China between 1983 and 1985.[16] Over 3000 factories in China use ICs manufactured by the #14 Factory. Similarly, Shanghai #19 Radio Factory manufactures TTL circuits and also has a large customer base, the majority of whom are defense end-users. The Shanghai #5 Components Factory has received several national science and technology awards, both the civilian and military, and is considered to be one of the premier producers of LSI chips (1K and 4K RAM) in China. The majority of the ICs manufactured in this facility are still at the medium-scale integration level. Since 1982, this factory has been designated as the experimentation and testing site (*zhongdian shiyan chang*) for IC production in Shanghai and vicinity.

In spite of the capabilities represented by these achievements, the industry has encountered serious problems when it has attempted to move into the design and production of relatively more complex chip structures. The Chinese have identified four problems explaining poor yields, low output figures, high prices, and uneven quality:

1. The low technological level of the manufacturing process
2. The obsolescence of equipment
3. The absence of a broad-based infrastructure and support system for the semiconductor industry (e.g. the poor quality of basic materials such as water and air, power shortage, etc.)
4. A number of economic problems[17]

Other reasons for the gap between research and production may be found in the overall nature of China's economic system and in a host of historical factors. (See Table 5–2.)

In some respects, these problems have caused Shanghai to lag even further behind international developments. One estimate in the local *Wen Hui Bao* in April 1987 suggested that the gap between Shanghai's IC production capabilities and the international state of the art had grown to eighteen years.[18] As requirements for achieving international competitiveness in microelectronics steadily increase particularly in the areas of capital, equipment, and design costs, the objectives of the Shanghai leadership to minimize imports, strengthen indigenous capabilities, and

Table 5–2. Technological State of the Art in Shanghai's Semiconductor Industry.

Basic Process	Technological Level	
	R&D (Field of Main Activity)	Production (Technique Mainly in Use)
Material	III–V compounds (e.g. GaAs), Silicon	Silicon
Circuit design	CAD	Handmade (partially CAD)
Wafer size	4-inch	3-inch diameter, 4-inch under preparation
Fabrication		
Etching	Plasma etching	Wet etching
Lithography	Electron beam	Optical method
Intro of dopants	Ion implantation, ion milling	Diffusion & ion implantation
Film deposition techniques	NA	Chemical vaporization (CVD)
Assembly	Automation	Semiautomated
Line width	3–4 microns	5–8 microns
Circuit density	LSI (VLSI under preparation)	SSI, MSI (partially LSI)
Yield rates	40–50 percent	12–25 percent

Sources: Personal communication, Shanghai, July 1985; various Chinese written sources.

eventually attain competitive status in foreign markets are becoming more difficult to achieve.

INNOVATION IN SHANGHAI'S SEMICONDUCTOR INDUSTRY

The development of new products and processes in Shanghai is initiated at many levels. Projects flow into the city by multiple channels, including the State Council electronics leading group in Beijing, the SSTC, the NDSTIC, the State Education Commission, the CAS, and such industrial ministries as the Ministry of Electronics, the State Commission of Machine-Building, and the Ministry of Space Industry. At the local level, projects are mainly initiated by the Shanghai Science and Technology Commission (STC) and the Industrial Bureau for Electronics and Instrumentation. In addition, a number of projects are self-initiated at the level of the work unit.

The details of Shanghai's current program for the development of new semiconductor and IC products and processes are contained in a series of long-, medium-, and short-term plans at the central government and municipality levels. The Bureau, corporations, and enterprises are all involved in the process. Self-initiated projects often come about as a result of contracts signed between research units and potential end-users—though these still remain relatively small in number.

It is important to note that in discussions of the innovation process, the Chinese make a sharp distinction between so-called new products that are in the realm of manufacturing and new technologies that are the focus of R&D efforts. The local Economic Commission assumes the main administrative responsibility for new products. New technology projects are initiated and managed through the local STC. For example, when research activities regarding the development of LSI technology were started in 1981 and 1982, the STC took the lead in funding and coordination. This separation of responsibility does not mean that the STC, for example, does not become involved in helping to support the development of new production processes. Rather, it is designed to ensure that the lines of authority are clearly spelled out to avoid possible jurisdictional clashes.

The role of the local STC is particularly interesting insofar as it frequently provides the main impetus for innovation-directed research activities. Among the numerous departments that compose the STC, several stand out:

1. Department of comprehensive planning, which plans and coordinates R&D tasks for the municipality.
2. Department for development and forecasting, which analyzes technological trends and does forecasting for Shanghai's S&T development at both the macro and sectoral levels.
3. Department for support and resources, which provides the financial and equipment support needed to undertake projects.

4. Department of personnel, which oversees the manpower needs of the commission. Even though the STC does have some responsibility for managing the city's S&T personnel needs, the local S&T Cadres Bureau is under the direct administration of the Shanghai Municipal Government.
5. Four functional departments (general industry, urban construction, agriculture and medicine, and new technologies).

The department for new technologies was created in response to the new emphasis given to emerging fields such as microelectronics and biotechnology. The STC contains a number of additional departments that come under its general jurisdiction mainly because there are no other appropriate homes for these offices in the city government. They include seismology, measurements and standards, birth control, and patents.

Projects generated by the Shanghai STC are planned in the following manner. First, the forecasting department receives a series of proposals from below and requirements from above concerning three areas: science and technology, economy, and social welfare. On the basis of this information, the department establishes a general framework that identifies priority research fields and projects. (The Chinese distinction between the *guihua*—which is a broad framework or outline—and the *jihua*—which is a very specific and detailed plan becomes important.) The most concrete manifestation of the forecasting department's activities is the elaboration of a municipal S&T development plan as the product of discussions with experts representing work units throughout Shanghai. The Planning Commission is then given a copy of the *guihua*. If it approves the general framework, the STC then gives it to its integrated planning department, which translates the *guihua* into a concrete plan with specific projects.

There is some feedback during this process. The designated representatives from the four functional departments offer suggestions, as part of the competition for funds. The suggestions go back into the *guihua* for consideration. Finally, each of the functional departments is given the responsibility for ensuring that the appropriate projects are assigned to the relevant units under its supervision. In the case of complex projects, several units may be involved. In the case of LSI, the municipal leading group for electronics has essentially taken responsibility for the entire process. However, once the projects are carried out and certified, many of the results never get into production because heretofore the research units have not adequately considered production. Moreover, the STC has not had the authority to force use of these results in production. The new S&T reforms are designed to change this situation. (See Chapter 6.)

Over the last several years, the locus of project initiation has increasingly shifted from the central to the local level.[19] However, while the market has come to play a more critical role in stimulating locally-initiated projects, a system of decentralized planning has steadily emerged. Guidance from above the enterprise level (e.g. the bureau, the local S&T Commission, etc.) is still a dominant, though not the only, source for promoting innovation. Second, even though more projects are actually being generated at the local level, the central government still plays a major tasking role through the issuance of tenders and bids. For example, the SSTC recently completed the evaluation of a number of alternate units for receipt of funds to carry out a research project on the application of gallium arsenide (GaAs) in ICs. Moreover, under the SSTC's "high-tech development program" it is anticipated that additional grants from the central government will be offered. Thus, while the number of lump sum grants from above may have diminished, the central government still structures a good deal of the innovative activity through the guidance it provides in announcing key national projects.

In theory, each of the specific innovation plans includes a project description, its financial sources, and a detailed time horizon for each step of the development process. The development process usually starts with a feasiblility analysis for the new product or technology and ends after the new technology or trial production has been introduced. In many cases, however, the process actually ends with a certification meeting, or *jiandinghui*, where various experts from the area provide their views about the stated performance of the new item(s). The new product or process is not often translated into production—primarily because the potential end-users were never intimately involved in its design during the initial formulation of the project. In addition, enterprise managers may have disincentives to introduce new technologies.[20]

The lack of a holistic approach combining research and production often means that many prototypes never enter the stage of mass production. Here the vertical barriers between different organizations and systems and even within the same unit have their greatest impact on the innovation process in China. Until now, when the Institute of Metallurgy, one of Shanghai's leading research institutes in the semiconductor area, developed the prototype of a new component, there was no guarantee that any manufacturer would produce it. The factory may argue that production is not profitable or that mass production requires too much adjustment within the enterprise. The factory also frequently lacks the equipment to produce the item and has little or no prospect of obtaining the foreign exchange to purchase it in the future. In such a case, the institute might then seek out an alternate production unit. Against this background, it is not surprising to find many institutes plagued by the "ends here phenomenon," that is, they are not very concerned about production considerations. In this particular case, researchers at the Institute of Metallurgy indicated that their primary goal is to master the research side of the innovation process.[21]

Even within a unit, organizational barriers can be pervasive. For example, among other reasons, loose coordination between the research and the production workshops in the Components Factory #5 thwarted attempts to produce a 16K RAM developed within the enterprise itself.[22] These examples are not unique. Each group or subunit feels responsibility only for a limited range of activities across the spectrum of the inovation process. Thus, since an overall approach is lacking, innovation efficiency tends to be very low.

Organizational difficulties are frequently accompanied by technological and economic problems. In the West, strong interrelationships exist between the semiconductor industry and end-users in developing both intermediate and final products. As Eric von Hippel has shown, while new technological developments in the components area have led to new applications and the creation of new markets, the needs of end-users have had a strong influence on the direction of innovation in the semiconductor industry.[23] As firms have attempted to respond to these new demands, equipment has been constantly upgraded and manufacturing technologies have steadily improved. Consequently, potential end-users receive the benefit of more and more sophisticated components at decreasing prices.

In some important respects, the role of market demand has been recognized by the Chinese, too.[24] Under the new production responsibility system, enterprise managers, in considering new product development, have been admonished to incorporate in their strategic analysis such factors as the forecasting of market developments, the consideration of customers' needs, the likely behavior of competitors, the assessment of competing products, and the evaluation of an enterprise's technological base for introducing a new product.[25] With the emphasis on profit retention that came about as a result of the October 1984 economic reforms, enterprises now have a material incentive to consider new products. This stands in sharp contrast to the past, when primary emphasis was on attaining production quotas. In effect, technology is now deemed an integral part of the Chinese competitive arsenal.

The actual picture among the enterprises and research units in Shanghai's components industry is still far from this ideal conception. Technological innovation continues to be primarily driven by technological opportunity and the desire for prestige rather than end-user demand, except when the Chinese military is the intended recipient. Similarly, despite the introduction of the Donghai 0520 microcomputer series, Shanghai's computer industry has yet to establish a strong market position because the semiconductor industry has not taken end-user needs into account when making design decisions. As a result, when innovations do emerge, they often appear under circumstances that are not sufficiently sensitive to existing technological and economic conditions are not given enough consideration. For instance, the prices of imported ICs are considerably lower than those manufactured domestically. And, given the general perception (and the reality) that domestic-made components are lacking in quality and reliability, even state subsidies that make these components competitive do not make them acceptable to customers.[26] Moreover, the concept of forward pricing, a strategic factor in the Western components industry which takes customer loyalty, future output, and increased market share as key price-determining elements, is not a factor of primary concern in the production of highly sophisticated components in Shanghai.[27]

Against this background, setting an economically rational price for a new component which is attractive to the developer, yet competitive with traditional products is not an easy task.[28] One advantage of introducing a new product or component is that there is considerable pricing flexibility in comparison with the production of existing products, whose price must conform to existing state guidelines. In the electronics industry, the innovation-pricing problem is compounded by the difficulty of convincing enterprise managers, who tend to be highly risk-averse, to introduce a new component—even one that constitutes an improvement—because chances are that it will initially cost more than an existing one.

With respect to developments for military applications, these types of problems are not so acute. The process of centralized tasking through the NDSTIC, which still dominates defense R&D efforts, apparently allows national security factors (e.g. the mastering of a new manufacturing technology or the successful development of a new component) to take priority over efficiency considerations. According to discussions with management personnel in the Bureau of Space Industry in Shanghai, defense research and production units operate on the basis of "cost plus 5.0 percent," thus ensuring a set profit no matter how long it takes or how much it costs to meet a task requirement. Moreover, the relationship between the developer and the end-users tends to be much closer, since projects are generally arranged from above and coordinated below by the local office of the NDSTIC or one of the other central defense-related organizations. The Shanghai Academy of Sciences (as distinguished from the Shanghai branch of the CAS), may also help to coordinate projects as well. The defense sector is not without innovation-related problems, but the Chinese still see centrally led government planning as a viable mechanism for promoting technological progress in critical areas.[29] And, as implied above, the development of sophisticated components such as LSI is viewed as an important national objective.

THE ROLE OF FOREIGN TECHNOLOGY
AND INVESTMENT

In keeping with the central government's principles regarding the "open door" and the catalytic role assigned to the import of foreign technology, Shanghai officials have stressed the need to acquire a significant quantity of foreign technology and equipment and to attract an appreciable level of foreign investment. From 1979 to 1987, Shanghai signed 282 agreements for the establishment of joint ventures (195), co-managed (84) and wholly foreign-owned enterprises (3). Direct foreign investment totalled US$2.2 billion, of which more than US$300 million was actually used. Hong Kong was the largest source of foreign investment, with 34.5 percent, while the U.S. share was 31.0 percent and Japan's 12.2 percent.[30] As of late 1986, over 80 joint ventures had gone into operation. Key examples of foreign-invested projects include the Shanghai Bell Telephone Company, the Shanghai Foxboro Instrument Factory, the Shanghai Volkswagen Automative Company, the Shanghai Squibb Pharmaceuticals Company, and the Shanghai Liftworks of the China Schindler Elevator Company.[31]

Similarly, foreign technology has been stressed as a means to support the upgrading of indigenous industries. Shanghai has been designated to receive a substantial portion of the funds allocated to the State Economic Commission (SEC) for import of 3000 technology items from 1986 to 1988.[32] It also received central government funds from 1983 to 1985, when the SEC administered a similar plan for importing 3000 key items.[33]

The primary responsibility for formulating technology import policy is in the hands of a municipal technology import group composed of members of the leading government organs in Shanghai.[34] The organization of the group reflects a division of labor along both a horizontal and a vertical axis. The vertical axis is composed of representatives from the main industrial bureaus and commissions; they are responsible for general planning, especially in relation to the technical and economic aspects of technology import projects. The horizontal axis is composed of persons primarily from the city's principal financial units such as the People's Bank. They are responsible for overseeing the financing aspects of the municipal technology acquisition plan. Five key organizations have been designated to implement Shanghai's technology import program:

1. Shanghai Foreign Trade Corporation, which mainly handles imports of machinery and equipment and related technology
2. Shanghai branch of the China National Machinery and Equipment Import/Export Corporation, which is primarily engaged in technology imports related to machinery and electrical equipment
3. China Jinshan Associated Trading Corporation, which mainly undertakes the import of technology in chemicals and pharmaceuticals
4. Shanghai Electronics Import and Export Corporation (SEIECO), which focuses on the acquisition of know-how and equipment related to electronics
5. Shanghai Investment and Trust Corporation, which handles all items not covered above, including the import of complete production lines.[35]

These entities all receive a service fee ranging from 1 to 2 percent for assisting with technology import work, e.g. linking the proposed recipient with a potential technology supplier. Complementing but not always cooperating with these local organizations are a series of centrally-led units with local branches, such as the Shanghai branches of the

China Electronics Import and Export Corporation and the China National Technology Import Corporation.

From 1983 to 1985, Shanghai concluded about 850 contracts for technology import, valued at US$870 million. According to preliminary estimates from Shanghai, foreign technology added an extra RMB 1.3 billion yuan to the city's gross production value in 1986; it is further estimated that total foreign technology imports will add approximately RMB 6.0 billion yuan to industrial output value and produce RMB 1.6 billion yuan in profits and taxes.[36] Technical renovation has been an important target for the import of foreign technology.[37] Close to 200 projects have been put into operation.[38]

Nonetheless, the acquisition of foreign technology in Shanghai has encountered problems. Difficulties such as duplication, inadequate personnel, and excessive expenditures of foreign exchange on spare parts and components have become very serious issues.[39] Still, the emphasis on technology imports will continue. At present, because China itself has only limited indigenous technological capabilities to create an advanced base for electronics development, Chinese leaders have determined that the acquisition of foreign state-of-the-art equipment is necessary to raise domestic production levels. During the Sixth Five Year Plan, China's electronics industry imported over 1,000 items of technology; one-third of the country's major electronics factories have been at least partially renovated through this channel.[40]

In keeping with this emphasis, the majority of Shanghai's leading consumer electronics producers and components manufacturers have acquired a wealth of modern, foreign equipment from Japan, the United States, and Western Europe. Between 1983 and 1985, Shanghai signed 168 contracts valued at RMB 144.0 million for technical renovation of its radio and television manufacturing industry. Approximately US$32.0 million was used to install fifty-two production lines, mainly for television picture tubes, washing machines, etc. For example, Shanghai's No. 1 Color TV Factory, producer of Gold Star brand color TVs, imported an assembly line and managerial expertise from Japan, and now can produce up to 400,000 color TVs annually.[41]

The components industry has been actively acquiring foreign technology and equipment as well. In design, it is clear that most of the ICs produced in Shanghai and in other parts of China are replications of foreign ICs. On the equipment side, the #14 Shanghai Radio Factory and the Shanghai #19 Radio Factory have both received advanced semiconductor manufacturing equipment from Japan and elsewhere.

For example, in 1985, Radio Factory #19 imported an entire IC packaging production line manufactured by Tabai of Japan. The line includes six inert ovens, three Fujiwa presses, two Fuji Seki blasting machines, and a Tabai Thermal Shock Chamber. Similarly, Radio Factory #14 imported a plasma oven from Plasmatherm of Sweden, microscopes from Nikon of West Germany and Bausch & Lomb of the United States, and packaging presses from Kotaki of Japan and Puscon of Hong Kong. While this equipment has made a substantial contribution to the modernization of the components industry, much of it tends to be seriously underutilized.

The reasons for technology import problems are manifold. According to one commentary in Shanghai's *Liberation Daily*, three major problems stand out: (1) a lack of industrial branch development plans to guide technology imports, with the result that emphasis is placed on short-term economic benefits to the neglect of long-term considerations and assimilation; (2) ineffective functioning of the technology import organizations and technology assimilation bodies, with a lack of coordination and unified command by an authoritative body; and (3) a shortage of funds to assist in assimilation, with the result that many key technology projects remain unfinished because of lack of funds.[42] We might also include a lack of understanding of the basic manufacturing techniques, the limited competence of engineers and technicians, maintenance problems, and the high degree of sophistication of the acquired equipment as important reasons for problems.[43] Moreover, because of controls on capital construction, there also have been problems with fitting newly acquired equipment into existing facilities, especially when many of these facilities are poorly suited to the requirements of efficient shop floor layout.

Problems in the effective use of foreign technology and equipment are compounded by the complex nature of the bureaucracy and the decision-making process associated with technology importation. Ironically, because Shanghai theoretically has a relatively high level of decision-making autonomy vis-à-vis the central government (US$5.0 million with respect to technology import and US$30 million with respect to foreign investment), one would expect the process to be somewhat more smooth and efficient. This is clearly not the case. A Chinese factory wishing to acquire a number of pieces of equipment from abroad must traverse an assortment of bureaucratic obstacles and meander through a maze of decision-making levels. One source has suggested that as many as 126 separate "chops," or approval stamps, may be needed for a project to be implemented in Shanghai. In Shanghai, factory managers frequently complain about the heavy weight of the municipal government, let alone the weight that the central government often brings to bear on decisions. One official described the process as an upward movement through "four stairwells and four steps in each stairwell." (See Figure 5–1.) The following discussion attempts to trace the decision-making process from the factory level up to the municipal government and central government levels in the electronics industry.

When a factory determines it wants to purchase equipment from abroad, the task becomes the responsibility of a factory subunit known as the technology introduction office (*jishu yinjin bangongshi*).[44] This office convenes an internal meeting that involves, among others, the chief engineer, the planning department, the finance department, the factory director, and the members of the introduction office. During this meeting, the role of the chief engineer is particularly important, since he must certify the technical appropriateness of the project. Once in agreement, the introduction office must then prepare two documents. One document is a proposal (*jianyishu*) that outlines the equipment to be imported, the alternative suppliers, the cost, and likely benefits; the other document is a feasibility study (*kexinxin baogao*)that shows how the projected costs and benefits were determined.[45] The document is then transmitted to the corporation's introduction office or project office (*xiangmu bangongshi*).

The documents pass through a similar review process within the corporation. Similar group discussion meetings are held and a recommendation is made. Even if the proposal involves an amount less than US$2 million, which is the theoretical level of autonomy for the corporation, it still must report to the Bureau—which can override or modify the decision. In such a case, the entire process may have to be conducted again. If the amount is over US$2 million, the Bureau must also provide its formal approval. Once within the Bureau organizational structure, the proposal becomes the responsibility of the import/export corporation, which in this case is the Shanghai Electronics Import/Export Corporation (SEIECO). Here again, even if the amount is below the US$5 million limit for the bureau, it too must report its decision to the municipal government's Foreign Trade Commission and to the central government—especially if the proposed import involves one of the newly controlled items, e.g. a television production line. Thus, even though Shanghai has a stated level of autonomy, it often must consult directly with the central government, which can intervene in the process if it feels that the terms are not in the national economic interest.

Figure 5–1.   Decision-Making Process for
Technology Imports in Shanghai.

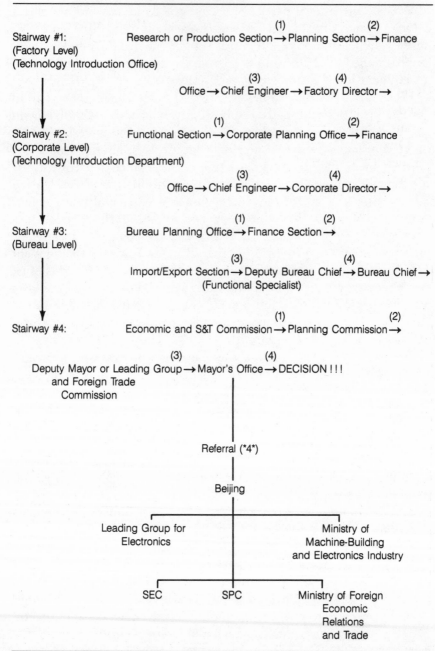

Stairway #1:   (1)   (2)
(Factory Level)   Research or Production Section → Planning Section → Finance
(Technology Introduction Office)

                            (3)   (4)
                    Office → Chief Engineer → Factory Director →

Stairway #2:   (1)   (2)
(Corporate Level)   Functional Section → Corporate Planning Office → Finance
(Technology Introduction Department)

                            (3)   (4)
                    Office → Chief Engineer → Corporate Director →

Stairway #3:   (1)   (2)
(Bureau Level)   Bureau Planning Office → Finance Section →

                            (3)   (4)
                Import/Export Section → Deputy Bureau Chief → Bureau Chief →
                            (Functional Specialist)

Stairway #4:   (1)   (2)
                    Economic and S&T Commission → Planning Commission →

                    (3)   (4)
Deputy Mayor or Leading Group → Mayor's Office → DECISION ! ! !
    and Foreign Trade
    Commission

                    Referral (*4*)

                    Beijing

    Leading Group for   Ministry of
    Electronics   Machine-Building
                                   and Electronics Industry

        SEC   SPC   Ministry of Foreign
                                Economic
                                Relations
                                and Trade

If a project is above the US$5 million level, it goes directly to the central government for review. Once such a project reaches the central government, it can be handled in a variety of ways. In the electronics industry, the MBEEI will have a major voice in determining whether the project will be approved, and if it is large enough, so will the State Council special leading group. Heretofore, if the proposed import involved production of a new item rather than equipment for technical transformation, the State Planning Commission had a primary voice in the decision. If the funds came from the budget for technical renovation, the State Economic Commission played a prominent role in the decision-making process.

Often, local units in Shanghai may try to avoid involving higher-level bodies. This is done in two ways. First, they may try to divide a project up into its component parts, thereby lessening the value of each respective agreement. Second, they may try to sequence the stages of a project. Both strategies try to give the appearance that an entire product or production line is not being imported. Monies for these projects can be obtained through five main sources: factory assets, the bureau or corporation, bank loans (which must be approved by the Bureau), funds for technical transformation provided by the central government to the municipal economic commission, and tenders by the central government.

SHANGHAI'S SILICON VALLEY: THE CASE OF CAOHEJING

In the early 1980s, the leaderships in Shanghai and Beijing became taken with the idea of creating a number of Silicon Valley-like sites in China. Underlying Chinese interest in this idea were the fabulous successes of places such as Route 128 in Massachusetts, California's Silicon Valley in Santa Clara County, and the Research Triangle in North Carolina. The more recent emergence of several imitations of the U.S. models in Japan (Tsukuba Science Park), in Taiwan (Hsinchu Science Park), and in South Korea (Daeduk Science Town) also stimulated Chinese interest in the concept of creating high-tech centers.[46] Chinese leaders believe that these parks will serve as technological hothouses, acting as catalysts for local innovation and technological advance.

From the history of the Silicon Valley concept in the United States, three points seem to stand out regarding the appearance and functioning of these sites and the firms that operate within them.[47] First, high-technology firms in such locations tend to operate on a rather different set of factors than other more traditional manufacturing firms. As Hall and Markusen suggest, the growth of these new high-technology centers is not based on those sectors associated with previously established traditional industries, but rather have been fueled by distinctly new forms of corporate organization and entrepreneurial behavior.[48] Most high-technology sites tend to develop and prosper in locations close to universities, government research institutes, and mature industries.[49] In addition, a well-developed infrastructure for adequate financial, personnel, and communications resources must be present. Dorfman, in her study of Route 128 in Massachusetts, has referred to these factors as "agglomeration externalities," whereby firms take advantage of the spatial concentration of certain industries and support systems in one well-defined area.[50]

Second, high-technology firms seem to require only a modified industrial infrastructure. They are not tied to a specific type of physical location, such as one near natural resources and energy. Instead, they are what one scholar has called "footloose industries;" they have a high degree of locational flexibility except for one main consideration—their need for highly skilled workers and scientific and technical staff members. Third, high-technology firms seem to seek out sites that provide a high quality of life, including ready access to cultural and educational resources.[51]

The roots of the creation of a Silicon Valley in Shanghai lie in a recognition among China's top economic and technological leaders that without spatial concentration, the establishment of a technologically advanced Chinese electronics industry would not be possible. This approach runs counter to much of Chinese thinking regarding industrial location over much of the last three decades; in the past, concentration of facilities was discouraged for reasons of national security. In order to reduce high investment costs, this new approach was viewed as pertinent only in areas which already possess an adequate technological infrastructure, an experienced and skilled personnel pool, a well-developed industrial sector, and suitable environmental conditions. Moreover, this approach is consistent with the new policy of emphasizing coastal development that was later announced in early 1988.

Against this background, a lively debate on the most appropriate site for China's Silicon Valley(s) developed during the 1983 to 1985 period, with many areas vying for designation as a potential site. From the beginning of the debate, there existed an overall consensus within the Chinese leadership that the areas of Beijing/Tianjin and Nanjing/Shanghai, due to their existing economic and technological capabilities, were the prime candidates.[52] Nonetheless, several other regions also attempted to be selected. For example, Shenzhen was initially proposed as a possible site because it had attracted a considerable number of newly established electronics manufacturing units and considerable foreign investment. Other factors cited included its geographical proximity to Hong Kong and Guangzhou and the availability of nonferrous and rare metals in Guangdong Province.[53] As of 1987, the central government had not made a formal decision on this proposal, though the development of the Shenzhen electronics industry remains one of Beijing's priorities.

In the summer of 1986, as a follow-up to the discussions during the previous two years, the concept of a Chinese Silicon Valley was formalized by the Ministry of Electronics. Based on the recognition that China did not have the financial nor the technological or the material means to set up several high-technology centers from scratch, it was decided to take the existing advantages of the well-developed coastal areas and to set up four major electronics S&T and manufacturing bases (sige jidi) to form the backbone for China's future electronics development. These bases are located in Beijing, Shanghai, Jiangsu, and Guangdong.

While the regional priorities of China's electronics development may be focused on the four bases, attention will also be paid to the so-called third line industrial facilities in the hinterland areas of Sichuan, Shaanxi, Gansu and Guizhou. These third line industries, most of which are defense-oriented, were specially set up in remote regions at a cost of some US$54 billion as part of China's efforts in the 1960s and 1970s to minimize the dangers of a Soviet attack.[54] The underlying reason for incorporating these third line industries into China's overall strategy for the electronics industry is that approximately two-thirds of the enterprises and about 21 percent of the research institutes which are supervised by the MEI are located in these four provinces. Most of these units continue to have strong military ties, especially within China's emerging missile and space program. In general, they possess considerable technological and economic strengths. Overall, they employ about 16 percent of the workers and staff of China's electronics industry (230,000 people), and they have received approximately 25 percent of the total investment into the development of the electronics sector.[55]

In some important respects, the economic performance of these units lags behind the rest of the Chinese economy. Labor productivity is only two-thirds that of most other sites, and profit remittances account for less than one-half of the corresponding figures for Jiangsu's electronics industry.[56] Since considerations regarding economic factors such as profits, productivity, prices, and quality have influenced the civilian orientation of the military sector, the question of integrating these plants with other segments of the electronics industry has received increasing support.

Within the "bases" concept, there will be a quasi-explicit division of labor. Beijing, because it is the workplace of over one-fourth of the S&T personnel in the electronics and information industries and because it has a high concentration of research institutes, universities, and production units, will focus on the development of advanced electronics technologies, including mainframe computers. Jiangsu, which recently established a cooperative electronics working group with MEI, while taking Wuxi and Nanjing as the base, will establish six electronics conglomerates (*jituan gongsi*) in order to expand significantly and comprehensively the role of electronics in the province's overall economy activity. Guangdong will establish itself as a major electronics export center, relying largely on consumer electronics. Conglomerates will be established in Guangzhou, Shenzhen, Zhuhai, Shantou, Foshan, and Jiangmen.

Shanghai's emphasis will be on microelectronics with the objective of meeting the component needs of the computer, communications, and consumer electronics industries. Another major thrust will be widespread application of electronics technology in transforming traditional industries. Ironically, the idea of creating a microelectronics center in Shanghai predates by several years the decision of the MEI to establish the "four bases." As early as 1982, Shanghai's STC began an attempt to give impetus to local LSI development by capitalizing on the presence of its key universities (e.g. the Institute of Microelectronics at Fudan University), well-trained pool of technical personnel, and large contingency of research institutes and production facilities.[57] Unfortunately, traditional rivalries over turf and jurisdiction between MEI, which tended to emphasize its own facilities, and Shanghai, whose electronics facilities are generally locally controlled, precluded any definite action in support of the concept.

By late 1984, however, the idea of a specific center focused on microelectronics re-emerged. In contrast to the preliminary discussions of the previous few years, this time Shanghai officials selected a specific site for the establishment of a high-technology zone in an area called Caohejing. From Shanghai's perspective, the Caohejing project was viewed as the city's most important effort to create an advanced semiconductor base. At its inception, based on central government policy developments, Shanghai officials thought of the Caohejing project as ostensibly a *national* project. To their chagrin, support, especially in financial terms, was not readily forthcoming from Beijing, which seemingly treated Caohejing as a *local* project. More specifically, MEI officials had begun to focus their attention on the potential of Wuxi, a site in Jiangsu province where MEI already had one of its leading R&D institutes (the Wuxi branch of the Sichuan Research Institute for Solid State ICs) and had already committed the resources to create a state-of-the-art bipolar IC production facility with imported technology (Jiangnan Radio Equipment Factory).[58]

The details of the Caohejing project remained vague because the financial issues lingered on for almost one year.[59] Some elements, however, are clear in terms of overall objectives. The basic premise of Caohejing was to bring together a number of Shanghai's research and production capabilities and mobilize them to work on semiconductor development. As a first step, the strategy called for the import of a 64K RAM production line (3 micron technology) to launch the effort;[60] the long-term goal for Caohejing was to establish a comprehensive high-technology zone where ICs, computers, industrial robots, biotechnology, and fiber optics would be developed and manufactured.[61] Initial investment was projected at approximately RMB Y 100 million, 80 percent from the Shanghai Municipal Government and 20 percent from the central government. Key participants in the project included the CAS Institute of Metallurgy (IoM), the Shanghai Components Factory #5, and the Shanghai Radio Factory #7, #14, and #19.[62] The precise division of labor between these various actors has remained unclear, reflecting, in part, the inability of the Shanghai authorities to produce and implement a well-articulated plan of action for the project.[63]

A key feature of the Caohejing zone has been the role assigned to foreign companies, both in technology transfer and foreign investment. The Shanghai authorities intend to authorize the establishment of eight or nine joint ventures. From their perspective, foreign corporations will make up for Shanghai's deficits in equipment, production know-how, and managerial expertise. A complete set of investment guidelines and incentives has been issued to attract foreigners. (See Appendix C.) A number of negotiations have taken place with companies from Japan (e.g., Hitachi), the United States (ATT), Holland (Philips), Belgium (ITT), and France.[64] As of early 1988, it appeared that both Philips and ITT would set up IC projects linked to the Caohejing zone.

The Caohejing project was originally formulated at a time when the precise relationship between the State Council leading group for electronics and its Shanghai counterpart had not yet been made clear. For one thing, the State Council leading group had recently undergone its own internal reorganization and readjustment and therefore was probably too preoccupied with sorting out its mission to intervene immediately. Similarly, the local leading group in Shanghai lacked the power to exert any direct influence on either MEI or the State Council leading group. While Shanghai officials, led by then-Mayor Wang Daohan, lobbied Beijing for support, the State Council remained silent.

After almost a year of contention about control over the project and its status, the State Council leading group apparently decided to assume some significant responsibility for helping to implement the Caohejing project and to coordinate it with other aspects of China's overall microelectronics development. This decision appears to have been a reflection of the leading group's willingness under its new leadership (Li Peng replaced Vice-Premier Wan Li as director in late 1984) to assume the role for which it had been created, that is, to overcome the parochial biases and regional barriers among key actors in the electronics industry and work towards the formulation and implementation of a coherent, well-articulated national electronics modernization strategy.[65]

That Caohejing became classified as a national project has important implications. Not only is it likely that adequate funds will be forthcoming, but this status also helps to facilitate the building of a critical mass of semiconductor specialists in Shanghai. And, in view of its prominence, Shanghai promises to have expanded access to advanced foreign technology—which might otherwise not be available due to foreign exchange limitations. Due to the considerable financial commitment of both the central government and the Shanghai municipality, one may also expect a stricter level of monitoring and control at each stage of implementation, thereby increasing the chances of overall success.[66]

On the other hand, the integration of the Caohejing project into the national strategy for setting up an advanced Chinese LSI industry was not fully welcomed at all levels of decision making, especially within the MEI. For example, the MEI preferred Wuxi as the site of a Silicon Valley. In June 1985, the Wuxi Joint Corporation for Microelectronics Research and Production (*Wuxi Wei Dianzi Keyan Shengchan Lianhe Gongsi*) was founded by MEI.[67] The new company specializes in research and manufacturing of all sorts of ICs, thus possibly becoming a major competitor for Shanghai. The decision to establish the four bases in 1986, including, in effect, both Wuxi and Shanghai, seemingly made this conflict irrelevant and preempted further development of such competition.[68]

The Caohejing project brought to the surface a number of the structural weaknesses within China's overall framework for managing its electronics development. It may be seen as an effort to gain new experiences for a product-related cooperation between different units. In this respect, it is a positive move forward as China attempts to create a modern electronics industry. Nonetheless, it is also clear that the envisaged effort will not be easily accomplished due to a combination of resource shortages and decision-making inconsistencies. Shanghai may have one of the strongest scientific and production bases for electronics in China, but it still lacks a significant number of critical elements needed to manufacture sophisticated components in large volume. These would include sufficient supplies of power, a well-developed communications network, and a continuous supply of competent personnel.

More important, the Caohejing project has also highlighted Shanghai leaders' very superficial conception of high-technology industry and what is required to stimulate its development. In a five-nation comparative study of high-technology industry in the West and Japan, Richard Nelson concludes that with respect to electronics the key factors were "a strong competitive market for domestic firms wherein technological prowess was rewarded and significant R&D support for firms in that market" was provided.[69] Underlying these factors was a coherent strategy characterized by rather clear and precise goals. In the case of Shanghai, up until recently, most of these elements have been missing, except perhaps at a very abstract, general level.

One reason has been a misconception of the California Silicon Valley experience in the United States. Silicon Valley and Route 128 were not planned but were created by the competitive market noted by Nelson. They have operated, for better or worse, under the auspices of that market. Governments may intervene, for example to absorb the start-up costs, as Taiwan, South Korea, and Japan have done, but ultimately the firm bears responsibility for maintaining a competitive edge. Another reason is the policymaking problems in China, both at the local level and national level. Vertical barriers combined with the difficulties of horizontal coordination—problems which the Chinese recognize as important—preclude effective policy formulation and implementation. Whether or not Caohejing represents a new step forward and is a product of what can be achieved under the aegis of China's multiple system reforms remains to be seen.

NOTES

1. For the general background see G. Dosi, *Technical Change and Industrial Transformation—The Theory and an Application to the Semiconductor Industry* (London: Macmillan, 1984).

2. Franco Malerba, *The Semiconductor Business* (Madison, Wisconsin: The University of Wisconsin Press, 1985), p. 18.

3. See F. Spital, "Gaining Market Share Advantage in the Semiconductor Industry By Lead Time in Innovation," Richard S. Rosenbloom, ed., *Research on Technological Innovation, Management and Policy,* Vol. 1 (Greenwich, Conn.: JAI Press, 1983), pp. 55–67.

4. Michael Borrus et al., "Trade and Development in the Semiconductor Industry: Japanese Challenge and American Response," in John Zysman and Laura Tyson, eds., *American Industry in International Competition* (Ithaca: Cornell University Press, 1983), pp. 142–248.

5. Daniel Okimoto et al., *Competitive Edge: The Semiconductor Industry in the US and Japan* (Stanford: Stanford University Press, 1984).

6. Shelley Tsantes, "Top Semi Companies: A Changing of the Guard," *Electronic Business,* March 1, 1986, pp. 78–80.

7. Ove Granstrand, "Some Basic Concepts and Models," in Ove Granstrand and J. Sigurdson, eds., *Technological and Industrial Policy in China and Europe* (Lund, Sweden: Research Policy Institute, 1981), p. 13.

8. For the most part, the reasons underlying this neglect of the commercial aspects is related to the military roots of the industry.

9. Wang Huquan, "Wo guo xin chanpin kaifa cunzai de zhuyao wenti" (Main Problems of the New Product Development in Our Country), *Keji Guanli Zixun,* no. 5 (1985): 26–28.

10. For a general discussion of the innovation process in the semiconductor industry see G. Dosi, *Technical Change and Industrial Transformation.*

11. Richard Conroy: "Technological Innovation in China's Recent Industrialization," *China Quarterly,* no. 97 (March 1984): 1–23.

12. Discussions in Shanghai, July 1985.

13. "Circuit Designer," *China Daily,* March 19, 1986.

14. "Development of a VLSI Design and Testing System," *Renmin Ribao,* June 6, 1987, p. 1.

15. See "Development of High Technology," in *Zhongguo Kexue Jishu Zhengce Zhinan,* pp. 136–138.

16. Interviews at Shanghai #14 Radio Factory, July 1985.

17. In one of the leading IC facilities in Shanghai, yield rates for LSI averaged about 20 to 25 percent for 1K and 4K RAMs. In the West, yield rates for such chips tend to be in the 90 percent plus range. Discussions in Shanghai, July 1985. See also "Famous Experts Discuss [Electronics] Development Plan," *Zhongguo Dianzi Bao,* August 15, 1986, p. 3.

18. "Speed Up the Pace of the Development of New Technologies," *Wenhui Bao,* April 11, 1987, p. 1.

19. Denis Fred Simon and Detlef Rehn, "Innovation in China's Semiconductor Components Industry: The Case of Shanghai," *Research Policy* (October 1987): 259–277.

20. "Yuan Baohua On Improving Enterprise Management," *Xinhua,* July 23, 1986, translated in *Foreign Broadcast Information Service—People's Republic of China,* July 28, 1986, pp. K23–24.

21. Discussions in Shanghai, July 1985.

22. Discussions in Shanghai, July 1985.

23. Eric Von Hippel, "The Dominant Role of the User in Semiconductor and Electronic Subassembly Process Innovation," *IEEE Transactions on Engineering Management,* vol. EM–24, no. 2 (May 1977): 60–71.

24. A concrete result of this recognition has been the appearance of so-called technology fairs, which ideally are aimed at bridging the gap between research and production. *China Reconstructs,* October 1985, pp. 26–28.

25. Deng Liqun, Yuan Baohua, eds., *Zhongguo Qive Guanli Baike Quan Shu* (Encyclopedia of Managment), vol. 1 (Beijing: Enterprise Management Publishing House, 1984), pp. 301–302.

26. See *China Daily,* December 7, 1985, p. 2.

27. M. Therese Flaherty, "Market Share, Technological Leadership, and Competition in International Semiconductor Markets," in Richard S. Rosenbloom, ed., *Research on Technological Innovation, Management and Policy,* pp. 69–102.

28. Hu Jinxiang, "Zhiding heli de xin chanpin jiage tuidong jishu jinbu" (The Etablishment of a Rational Price System for New Products Will Foster Technological Progress), *Kexuexue yu Kexue Jishu Guanli,* no. 10 (1984): 29–31.

29. One of the more interesting reforms that has been introduced has been an attempt to encourage the military sector to utilize its equipment, personnel and know-how to assist with civilian projects. The underlying motivation represents an effort to end the high degree of compartmentalization that previously separated military from civilian production and R&D units, thus forcing, directly and indirectly, the military to become more sensitive to efficiency factors. For example, see Yang Defu, "Jungong qiye zai guanli zhuna xing hou keji gongzuo de fangxiang yu mubiao" (The Orientation and Goals of S&T Work in Military Enterprises After Their Change of Management Methods), *Keyan Guanli,* no. 2 (April 1984): 47–49.

30. "Shanghai Seeks Larger Japanese Investments," *China Daily*, October 24, 1987, p. 4.
31. "Shanghai Solicits Foreign Funds," *China's Foreign Trade*, no. 6 (1986): 21–22.
32. "More Technology Imports Planned for 1986–88," *Jiefang Ribao*, November 27, 1985, p. 1.
33. A large percentage of the funds covered under the technical transformation program for technology import are in the form of low interest loans rather than grants. In addition, sometimes these loans are composed partly of RMB and foreign exchange dollars. On occasion, especially for important projects, foreign exchange loans may be repaid in the form of RMB. This amounts to a form of subsidy for high priority projects. Similarly, in order to ensure that a project reaches its stated export goals, the recipient may have to pay back a RMB/foreign exchange loan fully with foreign exchange earnings.
34. *Yinjin Jishu Gaizao Xianyou Qiye Jiaocheng* (A Course on Importing Technology to Transform Existing Enterprises). (Tianjin: Tianjin People's Publishing House, 1984), pp. 148–156.
35. Xiang Chongguang and Liu Guiyun, "Some Aspects of Shanghai's Importation of Technology," *Proceedings of Shanghai Conference on International Transfer of Technology*, Shanghai, February 23–27, 1984 (Shanghai: East China School of Politics and Law, 1984), pp. 42–55.
36. Li Zhiyong, "Shanghai Upgrades Traditional Industries with Imported Technologies," *New China Quarterly*, July 1987, pp. 27–31.
37. See the special issue on technical transformation in *Intertrade*, October 1985.
38. Xu Qinxiong, "Speeding Up Shanghai's Technical Renovation," *China's Foreign Trade*, no. 2 (1985): 13–14.
39. "A Noteworthy Issue: Digestion, Absorption and Renewal in Technology Importation as Viewed from Shanghai," *Renmin Ribao*, May 3, 1985, p. 2.
40. "Lu Dong on the Importation of Advanced Technology," *Xinhua*, January 16, 1986, translated in *Joint Publications Research Service—China Science and Technology 86-008*, March 1, 1986, p. 10.
41. Xu Qinxiong, "Speeding Up Shanghai's Technical Renovation," p. 14.
42. "Shanghai Improves Ability for Domestic Production of Imported Technologies," *Jiefang Ribao*, January 7, 1986, p. 1.
43. Technology import problems may also derive from external sources as well. In one facility, even though advanced equipment for the design of integrated circuits had been purchased, the software to operate these devices was not available due to export controls—thus necessitating Chinese technicians to waste considerable time and effort to develop the needed programs by themselves.
44. In some cases, aside from a small core staff, the members of the introduction office may rotate in and out depending on the tasks at hand.

Thus, staff members retain links to their functional departments, but are called upon to render their special expertise when needed.

45. The feasibility study generally contains eight sections: (1) basic data on the potential recipient; (2) information regarding the proposed technology; (3) data showing anticipated returns on investment; (4) an assessment of the raw materials needs and power requirements for the project; (5) an analysis of the potential environmental impact; (6) market analysis; (7) strategic assessment of the long-term value of the technology; and (8) a schedule.

46. Liu Zhenyuan, "Jiejian 'kexue gongyuan' jianli jishu kaifa zhongxin" (Strive to Learn the Concept of the Science Park and Establish Technology Development Centers), *Kexuexue Yu Kexue Jishu Guanli*, no. 5 (1983): 18–20.

47. U.S. Congress, Joint Economic Committee, *Location of High Technology Forms and Regional Economic Development* (Washington, D.C.: U.S. Government Printing Office, 1982).

48. Peter Hall and Ann Markusen, eds., *Silicon Landscapes* (Boston: Allen and Unwin, 1985).

49. Roger Miller and Marcel Cote, "Growing the Next Silicon Valley," *Harvard Business Review* (July/August 1985): 114–23.

50. Nancy Dorfman, "Route 128," The Development of a Regional High Technology Economy," *Research Policy*, no. 12 (1983): 229–316.

51. Craig Galbraith, "High Technology Location and Development: The Case of Orange County," *California Management Review* (Fall 1985): 98–109.

52. See, for example, the articles on the issue in *China Computerworld*. The debate started in mid 1983 with an article by Li Tieying, who pointed to Beijing and Shanghai as sites of the "silicon valley". See Li Tieying, "The Establishment Of Bases For the IC Industry Is a Strategic Question In the Development Of Our Industry," *China Computerworld*, no. 14 (July 20, 1983): 3.

53. "China's 'Silicon Valley' Should Be Built in Shenzhen," *Shenzhen Tequ Keji*, no. 2 (April–June 1985): 32, translated in *Joint Publications Research Service—China Economic Affairs 86-010*, pp. 123–124.

54. "Military Plants Return to Civilian Production," *China Daily*, January 7, 1988, p. 1.

55. "Talks Between Leading Members of the MEI and Four Provinces and Two Municipalities of Western China," *Zhongguo Dianzi Bao*, August 1, 1986, p. 1.

56. Ibid.

57. Included were the Institute of Metallurgy, the Shanghai Institute of Semiconductor Research, Fudan University, Jiaotong University, East China Normal University, the Shanghai S&T University, the Components Factory #5, and the Shanghai Radio Factories #7, 14, and 19. *Wenhui Bao*, July 8, 1983.

58. According to officials in Shanghai, one of Wuxi's major advantages versus Shanghai has been the absence of the degree of traffic congestion, air pollution, and water pollution that plagues the latter but not the former. In addition, many of the manufacturing facilities in Shanghai are old and obsolete, especially as far as the requirements of microelectronics are concerned.

59. Caohejing is located in an area southwest of Shanghai. The zone occupies an area of 170 hectares of land. It is 7 kilometers from Shanghai's Hongqiao Airport. Shanghai officials intend to build a number of office buildings, transport facilities, and residential buildings on the site. The decision to locate in Caohejing appears to reflect the desire of Shanghai officials to overcome the physical and environmental liabilities most frequently associated with that city in comparison with places such as Wuxi.

60. Intended capacity for this part of the project was 50 million ICs per year.

61. "The Construction of the Caohejing Microelectronics Zone," *Wenhui Bao,* September 27, 1986, p. 1.

62. Another indication of the central versus local tensions is the fact that the IoM essentially had to create a "new" entity, i.e. the 2nd branch of the IoM, in order to participate in the Caohejing project. Even the CAS in Beijing can become involved in the problems of *tiao tiao kuai kuai.*

63. For example, during mid-1985, there continued to be some uncertainty about whether Shanghai Radio Factory #19 would be involved in the project and what role it would play. One high-level manager from #14 had specifically been transferred to #19 to help facilitate that factory's involvement in the project only to find out later that the initial plans to include #19 were being re-evaluated.

64. *Wenhui Bao,* September 27, 1987, p. 1.

65. Based on interviews conducted in both Shanghai and Beijing, it appears that the MEI had come under criticism for pursuing policies that at the time reflected only its narrow self-interest.

66. Monies provided by the central government will most likely be in the form of loans rather than direct grants.

67. *Zhongguo Dianzi Bao* (China Electronics), July 30, 1985, p. 1.

68. In February 1986, it was announced that the Wuxi Jiangnan Radion Equipment Factory and the Shanghai Semiconductor Corporation will cooperate in disseminating 5-micron IC technology in Shanghai for use in consumer electronics products. See *Zhongguo Dianzi Bao,* February 25, 1986, p. 1.

69. Richard Nelson, *High Technology Policies: A Five Nation Comparison* (Washington, D.C.: American Enterprise Institute, 1984).

6 THE ROLE OF REFORM IN THE EVOLUTION OF SHANGHAI'S ELECTRONICS INDUSTRY

The experience of Shanghai's efforts to create a new basis for its present and future economic development highlights many of the systemic strengths and weaknesses of policymaking and policy implementation in China in general.[1] In particular, Shanghai's attempt to establish itself as a high-technology center has revealed the inherent tensions in central-local relations and the resource shortages that continue to plague the modernization drive. Since the early 1980s, the somewhat sluggish character of Shanghai's development pace—brought about, in large part, by both of the above factors—has evoked the concern of both central government and local officials, all of whom have recognized the critical role that this municipality plays in the overall Chinese economy. At stake, from the perspective of many of these leaders, was the future course of what heretofore had been China's strongest and most vibrant economic and technological base.

The need to respond to what was determined as early as Zhao Ziyang's visit to Shanghai in 1981 to be a series of fundamental and highly critical problems helped launch a major rethinking of Shanghai's development strategy.[2] Complementing increased attention and support from Beijing, a series of major reforms have been introduced in Shanghai to stimulate technological progress, improve industrial productivity, and set the stage for the emergence of new high-technology industries. In essence, Shanghai officials have sought to create an economic environment conducive to

145

more rapid and sustained technological innovation. In the case of electronics, this has meant both the use of government intervention and market forces to achieve desired goals.

S&T REFORM IN SHANGHAI'S ELECTRONICS INDUSTRY

Over the last several years, it has become increasingly clear to local officials that Shanghai's organizational and technological difficulties have frequently had economic roots. In the West, successful innovation and technological advance—in both intermediate and final products—has been characterized by strong interrelationships between manufacturers and end-users. In some important respects, the Chinese have recognized the role of market demand. One concrete result, the appearance of so-called technology markets, was discussed in Chapter 2. Under the new production responsibility system, enterprise managers in Shanghai, in considering new product development, have been admonished to incorporate into their strategic analysis such factors as product quality, the forecasting of market developments, the consideration of customers' needs, and the likely behaviour of competitors and the assessment of their products.[3] With the new emphasis on profit retention and other financial stimuli, they now have material incentives to consider the development of new products—a situation which stands in sharp contrast to the past when primary emphasis was on attaining production quotas.[4]

The actual picture among most of the enterprises and research units in Shanghai's electronics industry, however, is still far from attaining this ideal. For example, with respect to financial incentives, tax relief and tax exemptions have been introduced to stimulate the development of new products. However, exemptions and relief are only granted for a maximum period of two years which is often not long enough to succeed with a new product in the market.[5] It is, therefore, not surprising that the effects of tax policy measures on Shanghai's innovation policy are apparently still limited. According to an assessment carried out in seven industrial bureaus (probably including the Bureau for Electronics and Instrumentation) and 472 enterprises in Shanghai, tax relief and exemptions amounted to only 1.7 percent of the expenditures for new product development.[6]

In Shanghai, technological innovation has continued to be primarily driven by technological opportunity and the desire for prestige rather than end-user demand. Accordingly, when innovations do emerge, it is often under circumstances that are not always sufficiently sensitive to existing economic conditions, as discussed in Chapter 5.

The emergence of the research contract system and technology markets has begun to change this situation.[7] For Shanghai, the announcement of the Central Committee decision on S&T reform in March 1985 served to formalize a number of the experiments that had been introduced as early as 1981. Consistent with the thrust of the overall reform document, funding issues attracted the most attention. The introduction of a contract research system whereby R&D institutes would receive an increasingly smaller proportion of their funding from higher level bodies had important implications for both CAS-led units as well as Shanghai's local R&D units. By late 1985, the Shanghai S&T Commission had reported that 58 of the 803 applied S&T research units in the city had become partially financially independent;[8] by mid-1986, 19 of these units did not require any financial assistance from the government.[9] One leader in this regard has been the CAS Shanghai Institute of Silicate Research. Since March 1985, this institute signed more than 860 contracts for the transfer of technology and consulting.[10]

The newly introduced contract system has also been instrumental in facilitating closer links between Shanghai's military and civilian sectors. By mid-1986, the Shanghai Space Industry Bureau had set up twenty-six assembly lines for producing civilian goods. Many of these involved various electronics-related products, including radio and television sets, telecommunications equipment, computers, and electronics instrumentation.[11] Over the past two years, this bureau has signed more than 1100 technology contracts worth a total of more than RMB 17 million yuan. Overall, the NDSTIC-related departments in Shanghai have signed more than 3800 contracts and agreements for the transfer of technology from the defense to the civilian sector.[12] In spite of some resistance from the military with respect to the "surrendering" of time and effort away from their primary mission, the opening of the technology contract system has allowed them to increase their financial revenue and accelerate their own technological progress.

According to one article in the *Wen Hui Bao*, in 1985 the volume of technology sold in Shanghai through technology markets reached RMB 580 million yuan, a more than 400 percent increase over 1984.[13] This figure represents over 25 percent of the total value of sales made within technology markets throughout the entire country.[14] Although detailed statistical information about the role of technology markets for innovation of Shanghai's electronics industry is not available, the impact has been apparently quite considerable. For example, in 1983 and 1984 the Shanghai Components Factory #5, one of China's leading semiconductor producers, received about 50 percent of its research and productions tasks from the MEI, the State S&T Commission, and the Shanghai Bureau for Electronics and Instrumentation. As a result of the S&T and economic reforms, in 1985 around 90 percent of the factory's activities were self-initiated.[15]

The explosion of the volume of transactions handled through the technology market has been accompanied by a mushrooming of all sorts of consulting and development corporations. At present, there are more than 300 specialized organizations engaged in technology trading and services.[16] Shanghai's technology market consists of six different systems which handle the management of S&T commodities:[17]

1. Shanghai S&T Development and Exchange Center, which is subordinated to the local S&T Commission. It is the largest entity in the technology market. At present, it has thirty-four member corporations which are financed by the collective funds of scientists and technicians and which organize technical meetings, do consulting work, engineering and design and manpower training. In addition, the center together with S&T units in Shanghai has also set up seventeen technical development departments.
2. Shanghai S&T Consulting and Service Center of the S&T Association, under which there are 80 branch centers and 5 technical development corporations.
3. Universities and colleges, which have set up an S&T service center with forty-five technical service departments. Moreover, Fudan and Jiaotong University, the East China Chemical Institute, and eleven other universities have founded an S&T development corporation that utilizes the personnel and financial resources of these entities.
4. Local industrial bureaus, which have their own technical development and service institutions.
5. Centrally controlled units and the CAS, which operate a number of consulting and technical service corporations in Shanghai.
6. Collective/Private (minban) technical development institutions.

The rapid expansion of research contracts and technology markets since their introduction in 1984 is cited by the Chinese press as an evidence of the widespread acceptance of this new method of linking the research and production sectors. One source has suggested that prior to the introduction of these new mechanisms, only 20 to 30 percent of Shanghai's research achievements were transferred into production; by 1984, this source suggests that out of 1585 achievements, approximately 834 had been transferred—a remarkable increase given previous behavior.[18] In Shanghai in July 1985, it seemed that most of the research and production units indeed viewed technology markets as an excellent opportunity to realize higher financial revenues. On the other hand, interviewees also made clear that reliance on contracts and technology markets as a major funding source could not be achieved by administrative acts but would have to be integrated into a whole set of reform measures. During the first nine months of 1986, therefore, it was not surprising to find that the volume of transactions fell considerably; in some cases, the drop was almost 70 percent. The Shanghai S&T Development and Exchange Center experienced a 50 percent decline.[19] The main cause appears to have been excessive bureaucratic regulation. Measures to improve the workings of the market have been proposed, including making technology fairs permanent and decreasing their size, obtaining the support of specialized institutions for marketing R&D results or products, strengthening all forms of patent protection, and guaranteeing a reasonable level of financial support to the institutions.[20] Unfortunately, however, it will continue to be difficult translating these suggestions into actual policy as eradicating bureaucratic interference has proven to be more problematic than originally anticipated.

ECONOMIC AND ORGANIZATIONAL REFORMS IN SHANGHAI'S ELECTRONICS INDUSTRY

Technical Transformation

Economic reforms in the electronics industry are designed to improve substantially the technological performance and management of Chinese enterprises in the electronics sector and to give greater encouragement to the use of technology, both foreign and locally developed. The major reforms include the technical transformation of research institutes and factories. This program, which is administered by the local economic commission in Shanghai, provides financial support to modernize antiquated facilities and replace obsolete machinery with more modern, precision-oriented equipment and instrumentation.[21]

While the establishment of technology markets may be a means to promote innovation by giving market forces a more prominent role, technical transformation aims to upgrade the research and manufacturing base of Shanghai's electronics industry. Much of Shanghai's electronics industry equipment is of 1960s and early 1970s vintage. With respect to semiconductors, the reliability and yield problems persist because of the nature of the equipment in most facilities. As demands for better quality and more sophisticated products have grown in both the consumer and industrial electronics fields, the need for drastic technical improvements has become noticeable, especially as domestic producers have tried to compete with foreign suppliers.

Technical transformation of many of Shanghai's existing facilities lies at the heart of the economic reforms. In 1985, out of a total of RMB 3.56 billion yuan, RMB 2.50 billion yuan (70.2 percent) went into projects specifically dealing with technical transformation in Shanghai's industrial sector; RMB 259 million yuan (10.4 percent) went into supporting technical renovation in the electronics and communications industries.[22] In comparison with the electronics industries in other provinces and municipalities throughout China, Shanghai received the largest share of funds (14.5 percent). At the same time, Shanghai received only a very modest allocation for new capital construction in the electronics sector (5.6 percent of the overall outlays) in comparison with places such as Sichuan (19.8 percent) and Guangdong (18.9 percent).

In its most essential form, the technical transformation program is designed to provide factory managers the necessary tools to compete in the domestic and international market. The program includes a focus on the software as well as the hardware side of manufacturing. More specifically, it encompasses acquiring the know-how underlying improvements in prevailing manufacturing techniques and renovating facilities.[23] The basic goal is to modernize existing facilities through selected modifications and imports of equipment rather than constructing numerous new facilities from scratch.

Technical transformation includes a variety of additional measures. In order to change the existing product structure of the electronics industry, higher expenditures on R&D are necessary. The actual percentage of product sales used for R&D expenditures among Shanghai's electronics manufacturing enterprises is only roughly known. Within the framework of the Bureau for Electronics and Instrumentation, roughly 1 percent of the sales was spent for R&D in 1984.[24] Moreover, differences in research intensity among the various subsectors of Shanghai's electronics industry are reflected in different shares. For example, in 1983 funds spent for R&D and new product development by the Shanghai Broadcasting and TV Corporation amounted to only 0.39 percent of sales, while one of the leading components producers in Shanghai spent about 8 to 10 percent of the enterprise sales on research for new products and development of new production equipment in 1984.[25]

Another focus of technical transformation is the acquisition of new equipment. In Shanghai's electronics industry in 1984, regarding the investment in new equipment, the majority (RMB 175 million yuan) went to facilities manufacturing semiconductor components and parts rather than final products. Moreover, between 1983—the year the municipality started to introduce technical transformation measures into its electronics industry—and 1985, the city was provided with loans and grants equivalent to US$100 million for the purchase of foreign equipment, of which about US$50 million was spent for the IC (LSI) industry. Shanghai's main objective is to introduce new production techniques into the components sector. This would include, for example, the introduction of new ion implantation equipment that is capable of handling more complex chip structures than the diffusion-based equipment technique which is still widely in use.

Although all of these are important steps for improving the existing technological infrastructure in Shanghai's electronics sector, so far the results of these efforts have been modest at best. Despite the acquisition of a wealth of domestic and foreign equipment by Shanghai's leading semiconductor research and production units over the last few years, only modest manufacturing breakthroughs have been achieved.

The absence of an integrated approach with respect to equipment acquisition and assimilation is one important reason for the lack of substantial progress. The utilization efficiency of newly acquired equipment is highly dependent upon its integration with older equipment. To attain the fullest level of integration, a careful analysis of the existing technological capabilities in the enterprise is necessary. This analysis includes, for example, an assessment of the level of sophistication of the equipment in place, an appraisal of the educational level of the technical personnel, and an understanding of the requirements of mass-production compared with those of prototype development.

In spite of these requirements, most approaches at the enterprise level have been poorly coordinated and ad hoc. A 1986 article in Shanghai's *Liberation Daily* indicated that in a survey of 300 electronics factory managers, over 60 percent wanted to resign because of the uneven and irregular nature of the reforms and government policies.[26] This state of affairs has many causes. One is that many enterprises were forced to undertake wild spending sprees because they had to spend their foreign exchange allocation by a certain period or lose it. In addition, exogenous factors, such as export controls, affected the utilization efficiency. In one particular IC factory, an expensive piece of advanced CAD equipment imported from abroad to support mask-making was of limited utility because the necessary support software and peripheral equipment were subject to American export controls.

Other reasons for these problems, especially that of poor coordination, include the lack of a systems perspective on the acquisition and management of equipment. In addition, there is often no regular personnel training to take full advantage of the technical capabilities of the newly acquired equipment. Finally, the tendency of the Chinese to buy on the basis of price rather than quality can be a source of major problems, particularly in the market for used production equipment. All of these factors have resulted in the presence of a wide variety of equipment from different sources in Shanghai's leading electronics research and production units, therefore making it difficult to set up a well-organized, efficient production system.

Organizational Change and Decision-Making Reforms

Organization reform has become an integral element in Shanghai's new strategy for modernizing its electronics industry. In line with the 1985 decision of the MEI to decentralize day-to-day control over the management of its factories, Shanghai has also introduced a number of similar measures, all designed to facilitate the movement away from the central-local tensions of the past toward a functionally oriented, horizontally linked branch management system.[27] At the same time, discussions regarding the granting of greater autonomy to enterprise directors in Shanghai's electronics industry have also proceeded. These have been most clearly manifested in the decision announced in mid-1986 by Shanghai officials to disband almost all of the city's seventy-seven companies. According to one source, "without these companies, local enterprises can enjoy more decision-making powers."[28]

These changes could have important implications for the role of the central government in the activities of the local electronics industry. Most important, they will significantly affect the position and status of the industrial bureaus. The role of the industrial bureau in Shanghai's electronics industry, which has included oversight responsibilities for planning, research and production, will in all likelihood change in multiple ways as a result of the implementation of the organizational reforms. According to one source, the abolition of the vertical barriers of the system combined with the strengthening of horizontal linkages will ultimately lead, albeit gradually, to the placement of all electronics-related activities, including computer development and application, in the Shanghai area directly under the jurisdiction of the local industrial bureau. Within this context, the Bureau of Electronics and Instrumentation will play a dominant role in terms of macro-policymaking while micro-level management will eventually become the primary responsibility of the enterprises which are subordinated to the Bureau. Of course, as discussions in Shanghai in early 1988 indicated, engineering and implementing such changes will not be easy. Nonetheless, the overall intent is clear.

The future division of labor between the industrial bureau, the Shanghai leading group for electronics, and the local S&T commission may be such that planning and supervision of large projects which are of strategic importance to both China's and Shanghai's electronics industry, will remain under the authority of leading group and/or the S&T commission. Given the fact that organizational reform is most likely to proceed by increments, the leading group will still be needed to act in a way similar to Selznick's "organizational weapon;" in addition to setting priorities and goals for electronics, it will be called upon to coordinate, clarify, and overcome barriers that still exist in the system.[29] Meanwhile, the work of the industrial bureau will tend to be more locally oriented.[30] Moreover, in some respects, projects such as Caohejing, which proved so difficult to implement in the past, could prove more easy to manage under such a system where the issues of central-local control are designed to disappear.

As implied earlier, compared with Shanghai's newly evolving relationship with Beijing, however, the move towards a branch-oriented structure within Shanghai's electronics industry will probably be much more complicated. There have already been some problems with the delegation of authority to enterprises. A survey of 401 industrial enterprises in Shanghai, covering the electronics industry as well as several other sectors, revealed that very little decentralization of authority in medium and large enterprises had actually occurred. Three reasons were cited for this state of affairs. First, some local authorities simply do not wish to relinquish authority. Second, some large and medium size enterprises lack flexibility and cannot function under such "free" conditions. Finally, some supervisory departments do not completely comprehend the requirements of reform or the decentralization concept.[31] Out of 401 responses regarding the pace of decentralization, only in 3 percent (12) of the cases was more than 90 percent of decision-making authority effectively handed over to the enterprises; in almost 47 percent of the cases, only 60 percent or less of the authority for decision making had been decentralized.[32]

The exact details about the direction of the reorganization in Shanghai's electronics sector are still not fully known. Nonetheless, some signs to indicate the likely future direction of this reorganization have already begun to appear with respect to the emergence of several new industrial conglomerates. In early 1987, the vacuum tube corporation was reorganized into a new share-holding company called the Shanghai Electrical Vacuum Device Industrial Corporation (*Shanghai Zhenkong Dianzi Qijian Gufen Gongsi*). It is composed of the Shanghai Bulb Factory, the Shanghai Electronic Tube Factories (numbers 1, 2, and 4), and the Shanghai Picture Tube Glass Factory.[33] This new organization possesses an independent administrative and marketing power—though the precise degree of autonomy it has with respect to its relationship with the electronics and instrumentation bureau remains to be determined.

Perhaps even more of a sharp departure from the prevailing situation is represented by the creation of the Changjiang Computer Corporation in March 1987.[34] The new corporation will have nine key enterprises and research institutes as its nucleus, including the East China Computer Research Institute (also known as MEI Institute #32) and the (local) Shanghai Computer Factory. In all, it will join together forty-seven enterprises and institutes throughout the Shanghai Economic Zone region, with a staff of 41,000 workers, 12,000 of which will be S&T personnel. Its main purpose will be to develop the regional computer and information industries by pooling personnel and equipment resources. This is an important step forward, since Shanghai's computer industry has been plagued for many years by lack of adequate resources and coordination difficulties.

It appears that similar types of reorganization are also under way in Shanghai's automated instruments sector, the electro-mechanical measurement instruments sector, the scientific instruments sector, and the instruments, materials, and components sector. In all of these cases, amalgamated corporations are likely to emerge, each still linked with the municipal electronics and instrumentation bureau, but with much greater latitude in signing domestic contracts for the purchase and sale of goods and services.

One other development also deserves mention in this context, namely, the emergence of the so-called *minban gongsi*. These *minban* companies are collectively or individually owned enterprises usually founded by scientists or researchers who formerly worked in institutions run by the state at the central or local level, such as the Chinese Academy of Sciences. While the state does not provide the monies for investment, the funds needed to create these entities have generally come in the form of loans from banks. Some of the more promising endeavors have also received financing from companies such as China Venturetech, a Beijing-based venture capital company that is supported in part (40 percent of the start-up capital) by the State Science and Technology Commission.[35] The best known example is the Stone (Sitong) Computer Company in Beijing, which produces an IBM-compatible, Chinese language word processor.

In Shanghai, about 160 of these *minban* companies have been created; they employ more than 2000 workers.[36] Researchers and technicians account for over 40 percent of total staff, and R&D expenditures as a percentage of overall sales are generally above the 10 percent mark.[37] *Miniban* companies emerge mainly in fields such as microelectronics, biotechnology, computer software, and high polymers. A Shanghai scientist named Mei Wenyao, for example, within his minban company has developed an infrared optoelectronic switch reportedly superior to comparable Japanese switches.[38]

The importance of the *minban* companies for localities such as Shanghai lies in several areas. First, in many respects, the companies suggest that the locus of technological dynamism may be gradually shifting to include organizational entities outside of the traditional government apparatus. While they lack the capital and related resources that most formal state-linked organizations can access, the fact is that the *miniban* companies have much greater flexibility and are not constrained by the lingering rigidity associated with the planned economy. Second, because competition among them as well as with the state-led manufacturing and R&D units is intense, their lifeblood is their ability to innovate. In this regard, the *miniban* companies feel the direct pressures of the market on their everyday operations and cannot afford *not* to focus resources on innovation activities.

The rapid growth and increasing market power of these *minban* companies may be more than just an aberration. When viewed in conjunction with the formation of the larger computer and electronics conglomerates, their appearance may illustrate an important point about the Chinese system, both in terms of what has transpired in the past and what changes need to be instituted in the future. The management practices within these small companies reflect a great respect for persons with strong technical credentials; unlike the situation in many other enterprises, technical people are prized rather than subject to ostracism. Similarly, the *miniban* companies' marketing practices reflect a sensitivity to end-user needs and requirements, which also seems to represent a marked departure from previous practice. And like high-technology companies in the West, these companies exhibit a degree of flexibility and responsiveness that has been absent in China's economy. Of course, they have their fundamental weaknesses and may not survive the competition from the newly created conglomerates. Acknowledging this possibility, however, their experience may help point China's reformist leadership in the right direction, that is, away from excessive government interference on the economic and technological affairs of its R&D units and enterprises.

NOTES

1. See David Michael Lampton, ed., *Policy Implementation in Post-Mao China* (Berkeley: University of California Press, 1987).

2. See Mayor Jiang Zemin's report on Shanghai's Seventh FYP in *Wen Hui Bao*, May 5, 1986, pp. 1–3.

3. Deng Liqun and Yuan Baohua, eds., *Encyclopedia of Management*, vol. 1, pp. 301–302.

4. See the assorted articles in Jiang Yiwei, *Jingji Tizhi Gaige He Qiye Guanli Ruogan Wenti de Tantao* (An Inquiry Into Several Issues Concerning Reform of the Economic System and Enterprise Management) (Shanghai: People's Publishing House, 1985).

5. Wang Huquan, "Main Problems of the New Product Development in Our Country."

6. Ibid. Individual figures for the electronics industry were not available.

7. According to Shanghai's municipal S&T commission, the city completed 1585 research projects in 1984, applying 834 in production. A major

reason attributed to the improved application rate was the appearance of market-like forces, including fixed sum research contracts, joint research-production schemes, fees for technology transfers, etc. "Research Projects Profit from Reform," *China Daily*, March 12, 1985.

8. "Reform Pays in Science Management," *China Daily*, October 1, 1985.
9. "Shanghai Research Institutes Market Technology," *Xinhua*, March 13, 1986, translated in *Joint Publications Research Service—China Science and Technology 86-014*, April 21, 1986, p. 5.
10. Chen Renping, "The Position and Function of Technology Development in the Academy of Sciences," *Ziran Bianzhengfa Tongxun*, no. 6 (December 10, 1985): 1–4.
11. "Space Technology Spin-off Products Find Their Way to the Civilian Market," *Xinhua*, July 24, 1986, translated in *Joint Publications Research Service—China Economic Affairs 86-102*, September 10, 1986, pp.32–33.
12. "Shanghai Transfers Military Technology to the Civilian Sector," *Jiefang Ribao*, February 1, 1986, p. 1.
13. "Shanghai Technology Markets Are Prosperous with Great Economic Results," *Wenhui Bao*, March 11, 1986, p. 1.
14. *Guangming Ribao*, March 15, 1986, p. 1.
15. Discussions in Shanghai, July 1985.
16. "Three Features of Shanghai's Technology Market," *China Market*, August 1987, p. 25.
17. Jiang Dingguo, "Fazhan Jishu Shichang, Fanrong Jishu Maoyi," (Develop Technology Markets, Let Technology Trade Blossom), *Keji Guanli Zixun*, no. 7 (1985): 13–15.
18. "Advances in Hunan, Guangdong, and Shanghai Technology Markets," *Guangming Ribao*, December 6, 1985, p. 1. For a discussion about the poor performance of the R&D-production relationship see "City Fails to Apply Research," *China Daily*, June 22, 1984.
19. "Reasons Why Shanghai's Technology Markets Develop from Boom to Collapse," *Shijie Jingji Daobao*, October 6, 1986, p. 1.
20. "Reasons Why Technology Markets Shrink," *Wenhui Bao*, January 6, 1987, p. 2.
21. Concerning the situation in the components sector, see Hua Guangying and Xu Jiuwu, "How to Develop ICs at High Speed," *Guangming Ribao*, January 18, 1980.
22. State Statistical Bureau, *Statistical Yearbook of China* (Beijing: State Statistical Press, 1987).
23. "Trial Regulations for Technical Transformation in the Machine-building and Electronics Industry," in Li Boxi et al., *Zhongguo Jishu*

Gaizao Wenti Yanjiu (Analysis of the Problems Regarding China's Technical Transformation), vol. 2 (Shanxi: People's Publishing House, 1984), pp. 592–607.

24. Discussions in Shanghai, July 1985.
25. Chen Longsheng. "The Vigorous Development of the Communications, Broadcasting and TV Industries is a Strategic Task for Shanghai," in *Shanghai Jingji Fazhan Zhanlüe Wenti*, pp. 121–132.
26. "Managing a Factory Is Difficult," *Liberation Daily*, August 23, 1986, pp. 1, 3.
27. "Report of the MEI on the Enforcement of Reform of the Economic System in the Electronics Industry," *Zhongguo Dianzi Bao*, March 21, 1986, p. 2.
28. "Companies to Disband in Shanghai," *China Daily*, August 1, 1986, p. 3.
29. See Philip Selznick, *The Organizational Weapon* (New York, 1960). See also Philip Selznick, *Leadership in Administration* (New York: Harper & Row, 1957).
30. This regards in particular the projects which are initiated at the central level. Cf. Li Peng, "The electronics and information industries should serve the construction of the four modernizations."
31. "A Survey on the Delegation of Authority in Shanghai's Industrial Enterprises," *Liaowang*, no. 5 (February 3, 1986): 17–19.
32. Authority was measured according to fifteen categories, including such items as the power to set prices, the power to recruit personnel, the power to increase wages, the power to readjust plans, etc.
33. "Shanghai Creates the Electronic Vacuum Tube Shareholding Company," *Wenhui Bao*, January 7, 1987, p. 1.
34. "Changjiang Computer Corporation Founded in Shanghai," *Zhongguo Dianzi Bao*, April 3, 1987, p. 1.
35. It should be stressed that in China the concept of venture capital is different in both theory and practice from that in the West. In China, potential entrepreneurs get most of their capital from the state. In effect, it is a form of extra-budgetary funding. The biggest advantage of tapping this source of funds is that they can be provided more quickly, without going through a complex approval process within the PRC bureaucracy.
36. "Shanghai's 'Minban' S&T Organizations Enter a New Stage of Development," *Guangming Ribao*, February 2, 1988.
37. "Looking Inside at the Integration of S&T Reforms and Economic Reforms," *Renmin Ribao*, January 4, 1988, p. 3.
38. *Guangming Ribao*, February 2, 1988.

7 PROSPECTS AND CONCLUSIONS

In his study of the global semiconductor industry, Malerba suggests that "the analysis of high-technology industries . . . should not be placed within a static framework. Rather, it should include a dynamic, historic and evolutionary perspective that is able to grasp all aspects of the diversities and changes, continuities and discontinuities that play such a major role in all high-technology industries."[1] This holds especially true for Shanghai, a city in the process of trying to introduce major changes in the way its economy is structured and administered. Shanghai's effort to establish an advanced, well-functioning electronics industry poses some very difficult challenges for the local leadership. As this book has tried to show, Shanghai's ability to attain its objectives, especially in the microelectronics area, will be determined not merely through the import of foreign technology or other technical fixes. Rather, creating a high-technology base in Shanghai will require a fundamental transformation in ideology, management style, and organization. This holds true with respect to the relationship between the central government in Beijing and Shanghai; it also holds true for the relationships among various entities within Shanghai itself. Viewed from this perspective, while Deng Xiaoping's reform program is obviously important for all of China, it has special implications for Shanghai and will continue to do so for the rest of the century.

SHANGHAI'S ASSETS FOR PROMOTING
HIGH TECHNOLOGY

In a major study on industrial innovation in the Soviet Union, Amann and Cooper have suggested that "successful innovation appears to be associated with a high-level of government support—preferably of a longstanding and stable kind, low cost, average or below average research intensity, and low levels of 'complexity' in the sense of interdisciplinarity of research fields or close dependence on other industries."[2] Due to the Soviet Union's extensive influence on the development of China's economic and R&D system, it is likely that this hypothesis also applies to many industrial sectors in China. Yet, given the extent of complexity and the high level of research intensity associated with such industries as microelectronics, the prerequisites for successful innovation may be somewhat different. In particular, as Freeman and others have suggested, few technologies outside of microelectronics have the potential to alter the economy at both the macro and micro levels in such a far-reaching fashion.[3] Thus, there emerges the question of how the environment for innovation in such critical high-technology industries should be structured to optimize the value of the high level of government involvement that is normally associated with a planned economy.

There are many factors working in Shanghai's favor as it sets out to stimulate technological progress and promote innovation within its electronics industry. First, the leadership in the city is experienced. The fact that the party secretary, Jiang Zemin, who recently stepped down as mayor, was the former Minister of the Electronics Industry should not be underestimated. (His replacement as mayor [April 1988], Zhu Rongji, was the former vice-minister at the State Economic Commission.) While many people who were skeptical of Shanghai's new high-tech orientation may have been afraid that Jiang would overemphasize electronics, the opposite was true. If anything, he ensured that sufficient attention and resources were devoted to rehabilitating Shanghai's basic economic infrastructure as a prerequisite to the launching of any high-technology development strategy. Jiang also took electronics under his wing, making sure that the relations between MEI and Shanghai were on a better footing than in the past. Moreover, both the new mayor and Jiang are joined by a coterie of individuals, such as vice-mayor Liu Zhenyuan, who have a strong background in electronics-related R&D and production.

Second, the status of electronics is no longer ambiguous. Based on numerous announcements from the local leadership, electronics has been designated a frontier industry and thus is eligible to receive all sorts of special attention and treatment in the future. This designation, particularly as it relates to China's Seventh Five Year Plan, translates into more resources—financial, technological, and personnel—for electronics as well as more foreign exchange for the import of foreign technology. Key individuals in the State Council leading group for electronics also recognize the significance of Shanghai's capabilities and view anything less than a success as detrimental to China's overall economic welfare. Taken together, these two developments suggest that supports and encouragement will continue at the highest levels for promoting innovation in Shanghai's electronics industry.

Third, the push to raise the technological level of the electronics industry is being done through a focusing of existing and new resources rather than through a dispersed approach. The decision to move ahead on the Caohejing project represents a positive step because Shanghai's key research and production facilities will be working together towards a shared set of goals. These goals have been determined not through the vertical channels that operated in the past, but seemingly through careful discussion on a local, horizontal level. As the Caohejing experience develops further, it will not be surprising to see representatives from MSI and other ministries participating in the project. The move towards functionally based branch management should enhance the prospects for innovation within the environment being created by projects such as Caohejing zone.

The development of Shanghai's electronics capabilities is now viewed as integrally associated with the larger effort to develop the Shanghai Economic Zone in East Central China. (Although as of August 1988, China's State Council has abolished the Shanghai Economic Zone.) A broader set of intersectoral and intrasectoral linkages will likely be created. These linkages have the potential of providing a more pronounced stimulus for technological innovation, particularly in view of the newly acquired freedom that factories and research institutes now have to enter into contracts with one another. The move towards a wider focus also promises to break down some of the economic and technological blockades that have limited the diffusion of innovations. Uncertainties will remain regarding the full appropriability of the innovation process due to internal reverse-engineering and the immature nature of the patent system. But the increasing zone orientation of Shanghai will open up new vistas of opportunity and further enhance the resource base needed to launch and capture the benefits of innovations in microelectronics.

Finally, Shanghai's approach to building up a high technology industrial base has emphasized striking a proper balance between indigenous development efforts and foreign technology imports and investment. Previous problems with the inefficient and ineffective use of foreign technology have taught Shanghai leaders that successful assimilation requires a series of requisite domestic capabilities and resources. Moreover, if technological dependence is to be avoided, the capacity to adapt and innovate must be strengthened. According to the Shanghai's Seventh FYP, investment in science and technology is to increase at a faster pace than municipal revenues. This represents a significant commitment on the part of local officials to ensure that Shanghai retains its leading technological position within China. More important, it also reflects an emerging view of foreign technology as a catalyst to spur domestic innovation rather than as a replacement for it.

SHANGHAI'S SHORTCOMINGS FOR PROMOTING HIGH TECHNOLOGY

While Shanghai has made substantial progress in overcoming a number of the bottlenecks that previously inhibited or impeded innovation, several serious problems still have not been adequately addressed. Some of these problems have arisen because Shanghai officials are trying to create a high-technology structure on top of an old, relatively backward set of traditional industries. As the histories of most of the high-technology centers suggest, this often poses some difficult problems, particularly in terms of the skills possessed by the work force and the orientation of educational institutions. Hall and Markusen, in explaining some of the locational factors associated with high-technology development, indicate this even more forcefully when they state that ". . . new industries are growing where the old industries are not; declining industries, and the attitudes that go with them, appear positively repellent to the growth of new entrepreneurship."[4] Another set of Shanghai's problems has as much to do with the new policies as with the burdens of the past. These derive from the absence of a clear, well-articulated strategy for enacting and implementing needed reforms. In some cases, it is difficult to see how the pieces fit together; in other cases, the intended impact of the reforms is distorted by local parochialism or political factors.

These problems—both old and new—fall into four main categories: organization, research, production, and overall policy orientation. They are discussed below.

Organization

Although new reforms have been introduced, the *tiao tiao kuai kuai* problem has yet to disappear completely. There are still some tensions between the new MMBEI and the city of Shanghai *and* between those units run by central government ministries and those operated by the local government. The same holds true for the CAS and its relations with its Shanghai branch. As suggested, reforms, for better or worse, are tending to move ahead in an incremental fashion. They also are moving ahead unevenly, suggesting that progress in one area will not necessarily be accompanied by progress in all areas. It would be unrealistic to expect that over three decades of bureaucratic routine and precedent can be overcome in less than a decade. Nonetheless, these problems stand directly in the way of an overall improvement in technological and economic performance. They are system problems, i.e., the continued presence of multiple vertical barriers, and are not about to be ameliorated overnight by a simple decree from Beijing or Shanghai. As system problems, they affect economic behavior and the innovation process at both the micro and macro levels.

Because of the continued complexity of the bureaucracy and the involvement of numerous actors, the decision-making process regarding local investment decisions, foreign investment, and technology import continues to be long and complicated. In Shanghai a "one chop" office was set up under the new mayor to review and approve projects with foreign firms. Yet, despite attempts at streamlining and consolidation, the current State Council, for example, still comprises over forty ministries and commissions; this cumbersome bureaucratic structure is replicated, in one form or another, at the provincial and municipal level throughout China. Even with the reforms and attempts at bureaucratic consolidation made at the National People's Congress in April 1988, organizational impediments are ever present. At times, even participants within the system do not know the exact nature of the process or the criteria upon which decisions are made. Personal ties and *guanxi* relations still hold great weight, and uncertainty and delays are commonplace unless a factory manager has these ties. The process is aggravated by what one Chinese has suggested continues to be a widespread aspect of the system, namely that "those who have authority do not want responsibility and those who will accept responsibility do not have any authority." And, as recent reports in the Western press indicate, these factors pose serious barriers in negotiations with foreigners who wish to do business in cities such as Shanghai. While Shanghai may be somewhat better off than other cities in China, the institutionalization of economic and technology-related decision making still has a long way to go before greater efficiency and objectivity will become an inherent part of the policy process.

Since the early 1980s, numerous new organizational entities have been created in Shanghai in order to promote innovation and technology transfer. These two tasks in the past frequently proved difficult and time-consuming because of the cumbersome nature of the local bureaucracy. While in theory the creation of new organizations for these purposes has generally been a positive step, the results have been less favorable than anticipated. A good example is the experience of the Shanghai leading group for electronics. A basic characteristic of the Chinese system is that without direct access to or control over funding, an organization's power and influence are very limited *(meiyou qian meiyou quan)*. The Shanghai leading group does not have a budget of its own and therefore cannot directly exert the type of influence necessary to accomplish its objectives. Thus, it has usually continued to play a less than optimal role given its mandate. These types of ambiguities must be cleared up if new organizational forms are to be able to accomplish their primary missions.

Last, in spite of the clear intention of some organizational reforms, uncertainty continues over the goals of innovation, especially at the micro level. Under the economic reforms, profits are supposed to be one of the main motivating forces for managers. Yet, in a system that for three decades was concerned primarily with maximizing social welfare and acting on behalf of the collective good, the new tendency of R&D units, enterprises, and even individual persons to act in pursuit of self-aggrandizement has not always been viewed in a positive light. Moreover, the drive for profitability has produced a lot of short-term thinking among Shanghai managers, leading some actually to ignore the potential for innovation or technological advance. This is especially problematic in consumer electronics, where demand often exceeds supply and hence pressures for quality-related improvements or product diversification are often absent.

A similar argument can be made regarding the spending of foreign exchange to support innovation and technological upgrading. In many cases, and with some notable exceptions, foreign exchange constraints severely limit the ability of researchers and engineers to acquire the equipment they need to develop new products or improve existing ones. Most acquisition decisions are based on price rather than quality; while this is not surprising in a system that is plagued by a scarcity of foreign exchange, it often leads Chinese buyers to focus on hardware rather than software and forces them to neglect purchases of such crucial items as maintenance and service agreements. Moreover, the back-and-forth movement regarding decision-making autonomy tends to force managers to spend their money as rapidly as possible once they have it rather than spend in a more incremental, directed fashion. As a result, support for innovation still has a low priority for many managers, the majority of whom are looking to maximize immediate opportunities. Shanghai's bad experience in the early 1980s with massive influx of personal computer kits (many of which were IBM PCs) from Hong King illustrates how short-term thinking can have very deleterious effects. In this case, the rush to earn a profit from the assembly of imported PC kits nearly destroyed the local computer base in Shanghai; its impact on local innovation was extremely deleterious.

Research and Development

Many new reforms have been introduced into the R&D system to improve innovative performance and create better links between research and production. As suggested, these have all generally had a very positive impact on the innovation process and the movement of R&D results to potential end-users. The problem, in some cases, is that they have not gone far enough fast enough. The creation of the Caoheijing project, while a step in the right direction, still represents the continued attempt to use top-down mechanisms to promote technological innovation. Because of the continued efficacy of administrative barriers, the establishment of science-production associations in the USSR created, in many instances, a mechanical conglomerate of independent organizations rather than entities responsive to the changing economic environment. Such too is the potential outcome in the case of Shanghai. As the economic environment changes, more leeway has to be given to grassroots efforts as the primary mechanism to achieve the city's technological goals. Otherwise, a somewhat artificial character will continue to dominate these types of endeavors. Similarly, until the economic signals being received by managers begin to change, new technology will be seen as a risk and even an inconvenience rather than as a potential asset.

These points suggest that the future path and pace of innovation in Shanghai's electronics industry will depend much on what is done with respect to such issues as price reform, the issuance of standards and quality control requirements, and the degree of protectionism within the Chinese market—with respect to both cross-provincial sales and foreign imports. A recent effort seemingly championed by newly elected Premier Li Peng, seeks to impose new controls on the import of foreign components and final electronics products because of growing concerns that the presence of foreign products is undermining domestic development and inhibiting local R&D. While there may be some merits to this argument, the competition may be the most valuable lever that Chinese officials can push in order to stimulate innovative behavior. As the experience with import substitution in many of Latin America's developing nations has shown, excessive protection of the local market, without proper sequencing and support, could seriously hinder innovation.

This is not to suggest that the local Shanghai government and the central government do not have an important role to play in the R&D system. In fact, the creation of the leading groups in Shanghai and in Beijing suggests that places such as Shanghai will be following a two-pronged strategy. Moreover, Hall and Markusen's work on regionally-oriented, high-technology development strategies stresses the need for coordination between the roles of government and the market. Thus, on the one hand, the Chinese will rely on market forces, to some extent, to drive production of consumer electronics and further product development in this area. On the other hand, the local government, in conjunction with Beijing, will provide direct support for major initiatives such as the R&D aspects of Caohejing in order to create synergies where the immaturity of market forces in China might not naturally bring certain actors together. The problem is that, for both economic and socio-political reasons, there continue to be too many interventions to allow market forces to mature—and thus the top-down approach continues to predominate in almost all sectors.

Specific problems have appeared at the institute level in Shanghai regarding the effort by the central government to establish greater financial independence at the working level. Although this policy was partially instituted, it has created greater anxiety among many research units because the exact impact and meaning of the policy remains somewhat uncertain. A sizable number of research institutes in Shanghai and elsewhere have responded to this pressure by establishing their own production facilities; in several respects, the growing number of these new facilities seems to portend a distinct move away from research in these institutes as they cannot find willing enterprise managers to buy their new ideas and products.

In some ways, Chinese expectations of their own research institutes regarding the matter of financial independence are extremely overambitious. Breaking down the "iron rice bowl" of the past where funding was guaranteed and performance was generally ignored is a positive development. However, an appreciable percentage of Shanghai's institutes in the electronics sector do not have the talent or the marketing savvy to stand on their own. In many cases, it is not simply a problem of their being deficient; rather, their lack of responsiveness to the new policies derives from the fact that they are a product of the old system and need to be given the incentives to wean themselves away from dependence on old ways of doing things. Unfortunately, the unevenness in the pace and scope of the economic reforms has made this transition more difficult and uncertain.

Production

The problems of underutilization of equipment and poor systems integration have been highlighted. Shanghai's ability to meet its equipment and technology needs is extremely limited by foreign exchange constraints. These do not promise to disappear soon, unless the city develops into a major export earner. However, Shanghai could make substantial progress by focusing more attention on the basics of production: in plant management, i.e. inventory control and scheduling; in manufacturing management, i.e. quality control, maintenance; in the availability of spare parts; and in the management of skilled personnel. The reliability of raw material and components suppliers must also be improved. IC production in Shanghai is frequently interrupted by the absence of adequate numbers of wafers for chip manufacturing or the breakdown of machinery and instrumentation due to poor maintenance or limited user capabilities. Inadequate supplies of power are also a serious problem.

Factory management in Shanghai seems to be improving. New persons with technical credentials, many in the thirty-five to forty-five age category, are replacing people who gained their positions as a result of the Cultural Revolution or personal ties. These improvements have taken place in less than a decade. At the same time, a new type of tension has emerged because many of the new managers are former engineers—some actually have been former chief engineers in their factories. As Wells pointed out in his study of Indonesia, there is a tension between "economic man" and "engineering man," with the latter emphasizing technology and the former emphasizing cost consideration.[5] In an economy with unclear signals, it is difficult for a manager to know where and when to optimize technology or cost. This has important implications for the training of new managers in places such as Fudan University, where a new management school has been established and a program for technology management created. Simply put, the trouble is that the prescriptive element in such management training programs tends to leave students with many doubts about which principles, socialist or capitalist, they should follow.

Production problems in Shanghai's electronics industry also emanate from the absence of a true learning curve. It remains very difficult for Shanghai officials to determine future directions based on past or current behavior. While the market is indeed more important than in the past, many goals are still set outside the production unit. Distribution channels remain circumscribed in many instances, by the continued efficacy of the planned economy with all of its historically derived distortions. In large part, markets still are not yet the driving factor behind most production-related decisions in factories. Thus, the possibility of creating national economies of scale is more of a future goal than a present reality because there remain various obstacles to the operation of open markets in the domestic economy. All of this translates into continued confusion regarding production orientation, scale, quality, etc. The implications for innovative behavior are obvious.

Overall Policy Issues

The problems with innovation in Shanghai's electronics industry are representative of many of the problems being experienced in other parts of China's electronics industry. They are also very similar to many of the general problems being experienced in other areas of the country as a result of the incomplete nature of economic reform. The impact of this incompleteness has fallen directly on the shoulders of managers in both the research system and production system. The source of many of the problems lies at the policy making level and at the enterprise and institute level.

China's inability heretofore to put forth a coherent strategy for national electronics and computer development has been the most serious problem faced by Shanghai's electronics industry. Without a clear program at the center for electronics development, the funds necessary to support Shanghai have not been forthcoming. Even after the announcement of the four bases concept, some ambiguity continues to exist. Unless top leaders such as newly appointed Party Secretary Zhao Ziyang and Premier Li Peng push for changes in the policymaking apparatus, needed reforms will not be introduced and Chinese policymaking for electronics will continue to be beset by bureaucratic, rather than market, competition. The decision, forced upon MEI in some respect, to decentralize management of its enterprises represents a step in the right direction, but even in this case, many questions remain about the status of so-called *xiafang* units. Do they belong to the local government? Do they still belong to MMBEI? Are they really independent operating units? How do they relate to so-called local entities, such as the industrial bureaus? In many cases, actions are taken at the policy level without thinking about their implications or the likely implementation distortions that might occur. It is still unclear whether China indeed has an overall strategy for reform, one that can be tailored to deal with the types of problems that are confronting the electronics sector.

The appointment of Li Tieying as the Minister of MEI in 1985 and as Director of the State Council Economic Restructuring Commission approximately eighteen months later was considered by many to be a step forward. Based on his experience in Liaoning province, Li was thought to be sufficiently sensitive to the problems experienced by cities such as Shanghai. Nonetheless, his programs for the restructuring and streamlining of the electronics industry too became vulnerable insofar as they depended on the existing bureaucracy. Since several ministries are involved in electronics-related research, production, and application activities, an individual ministry can no longer focus exclusively on protecting its own interests—this would damage efforts at greater coordination and cooperation. New incentives had to be created to lure MEI in this direction. Heretofore, MEI preferred to focus on new products in the highly profitable consumer electronics segment of the industry.

At times, this has led it to refrain from supporting price reforms in such areas as housing, food and clothing that could alter the disposable income available to potential customers of its products.

The decision by the top leadership during the Seventh NPC in April 1988 to merge the MEI with the State Machine-Building Commission appears entirely consistent with these themes.[6] The new organization, tentatively named the Ministry of Machine-Building and Electronics Industry, is in some respects a super-ministry. It represents the coming together of two of the most powerful ministerial entities in the Chinese bureaucracy. In addition, it reflects China's desire to follow the Japanese lead in focusing on developing the field of mechatronics, a synthesis of mechanical and electronic engineering. Through the integration of these two technologies new technologies have emerged, including robotics, office automation, smart mechanisms, and advanced machine tools for use in computer-aided and computer-integrated manufacturing.

Interestingly, the creation of this new, comprehensive ministry occurred after a fascinating debate within the leadership regarding the merits of moving in a different direction, namely, forming an "informatics ministry" that would have combined MEI and the Ministry of Posts and Telecommunications. This proposal was ultimately rejected for a number of reasons, a key one being that the MPT, which strongly opposed the suggestion, apparently won its argument that it is primarily a "service" and not manufacturing entity and that every major country has a separate agency for handling postal and communication affairs. In reality, implementation of this proposal would have joined two ministries whose past relations have been often characterized by extreme competition and even animosity.

In keeping with the trends in the past in this industry, the merger contains measures for further streamlining the electronics bureaucracy. Out of the five functional departments, only three—computers, microelectronics and components, and broadcasting and television—will be moved over. See Figure 7–1. In addition, only 25 to 30 percent of the MEI staff will assume positions in the new organization. The remaining staff apparently will be placed in eight to ten new companies that will be created specifically for handling various aspects of the electronics industry. One of these new organizations, for example, will be charged with assisting in the financing of medium and large computer and related projects. Most of the changes seem to constitute a further substantial deepening of the reforms and divestment of authority. Nonetheless, it remains to be seen whether these new companies will

Figure 7-1. Ministry of Machine-Building and Electronics Industry

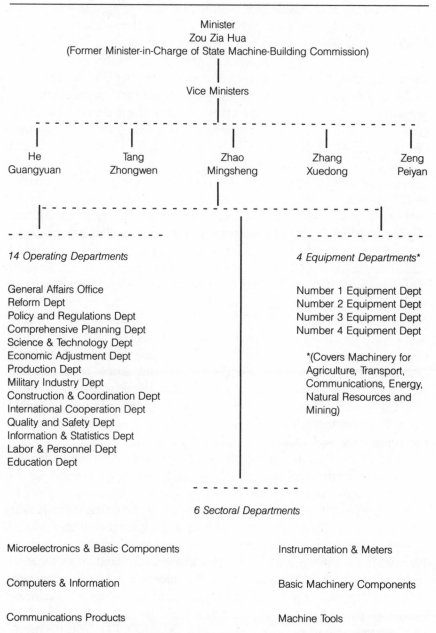

Minister
Zou Zia Hua
(Former Minister-in-Charge of State Machine-Building Commission)

Vice Ministers

| He Guangyuan | Tang Zhongwen | Zhao Mingsheng | Zhang Xuedong | Zeng Peiyan |

14 Operating Departments

General Affairs Office
Reform Dept
Policy and Regulations Dept
Comprehensive Planning Dept
Science & Technology Dept
Economic Adjustment Dept
Production Dept
Military Industry Dept
Construction & Coordination Dept
International Cooperation Dept
Quality and Safety Dept
Information & Statistics Dept
Labor & Personnel Dept
Education Dept

4 Equipment Departments*

Number 1 Equipment Dept
Number 2 Equipment Dept
Number 3 Equipment Dept
Number 4 Equipment Dept

*(Covers Machinery for Agriculture, Transport, Communications, Energy, Natural Resources and Mining)

6 Sectoral Departments

Microelectronics & Basic Components

Computers & Information

Communications Products

Instrumentation & Meters

Basic Machinery Components

Machine Tools

Source: Zhongguo Dianzi Bao (China Electronics News), May 3, 1988.

merely constitute "old wine in new bottles" or truly represent a marked departure from the prevailing system of administration.

The setting of technological priorities also remains a serious problem. Shanghai has become embroiled in the debate about what level of electronics technology is most appropriate for the country. The decision to embark upon a 64K DRAM production facility in Caohejing seems realistic, but the Chinese must also consider the fact that this decision was made almost three years ago. Since then major changes— especially technological—have taken place in the international semiconductor industry. If the most attention is directed toward consumer electronics, 64K technology may provide the key to entering the world export market in the low to medium end of the electronics industry. However, it will not give China the technological wherewithal it needs to remain competitive over a sustained period of time.

This may not be so bad. Gradual progress appears to be entirely appropriate for China, especially given its huge, still relatively untapped domestic market. Many advanced electronics products can be designed and manufactured with 1970s and early 1980s technology. Under such circumstances, it is not radical innovation that should occupy the attention of the Chinese; incremental innovation is what is needed. The problem for China is to be able to do this well so that product quality and reliability are no longer such outstanding issues. This is an important policy issue because Beijing has tended to push too hard on achieving advanced technological levels without providing ample resources and support for basic improvements in the production infrastructure. While this has begun to change, as witnessed by the increased funds available for technical transformation, it still has far to go before China's manufacturing base will be able to meet international standards.

As for Shanghai, the implications are quite clear. Shanghai officials have evidenced that they understand the nature of their innovation problems; they may even understand the nature of the tradeoffs involved in addressing fundamental, long-term issues as opposed to trying to make a technological leap forward without having a sufficient education, R&D and production foundation in place. In order for Shanghai to improve its climate for innovation and thereby achieve its stated goals for electronics, it must better integrate multiple elements of its development strategy. Moreover, there should be better feedback systems established in areas such as technology import, so that the experience of others can be used to assist future recipients of technology. Similarly, the newly emerging bureaucracy for foreign investment in Shanghai must not spend most of its time on attracting foreign firms without paying sufficient attention to the linkages between joint ventures and the city's broader modernization objectives.

In the final analysis, Shanghai will, in all likelihood, establish its role as a center for electronics and computer development in China. New pressures and channels for innovation will increasingly make themselves felt. In this regard, we can be cautiously optimistic. The optimism comes from the extent to which changes have been made in recent years and the high level of commitment among the top leaders. The Chinese experience with promoting innovation in the Shanghai semiconductor industry suggests that while the microelectronics revolution may be largely technology-driven, its development in planned economies must be accompanied by various forms of structural change. This structural change must be aimed principally, though not entirely, at altering the role of government, which may be in the best position to absorb the start-up costs at the early inception of the industry, but which also must give way at a later point to the market to ensure continued innovation and progress.

In highlighting the critical role that government plays in the promotion of high-technology industries like microelectronics, we do not deny the technological bottlenecks that the Chinese face in such areas as circuit design and chip manufacture. These are indeed significant problems for new entrants, especially as the complexity of chip architecture increases and the associated equipment requirements climb. Nonetheless, we believe that particularly in planned societies, the main obstacles to innovation have more to do with the arrangement of the key parts of the innovation process and the criteria by which they relate to one another rather than to the presence (or absence) of any one piece of equipment or mastery of any one specific facet of technical know-how.

Without a doubt, electronics will be a leading sector in China's economy; through a combination of nurturing from the top and increased entrepreneurship on the part of China's emerging cadre of high-quality managers and researchers, it promises to be one of the pockets of excellence in the economy. As a core technology sector, the development of electronics will also help strengthen China's ability to make progress in other fields, such as machine tools, automobiles, telecommunications, etc. It may eventually become one of the wedges that the Chinese use to establish a presence in the world economy. The integration of the electronics ministry with the machine-building commission will help make this a reality. At the very least, foreign firms will have the opportunity to form a variety of transnational linkages with China's research sector. This opportunity could yield a sustained access to a steadily improving stream of new ideas and engineering know-how.

The caution comes from continued evidence of obstructionism and lethargy regarding many of these new policies. While Shanghai's electronics modernization may not be seriously disrupted, it could be slowed down if this obstructionism cannot be overcome. Whether or not this can be achieved relatively quickly remains to be seen. Small successes will breed larger ones. Then again, Shanghai has a long history and a number of vested interests that see reform and innovation as threats to their own positions and status. As such, the verdict on the future must, of necessity, still remain somewhat uncertain.

NOTES

1. Franco Malerba, *The Semiconductor Business* (Madison: University of Wisconsin Press, 1985), p. 240.
2. Ronald Amann, "Industrial Innovation in the Soviet Union: Methodological Perspectives and Conclusions," in Ronald Amann and J.M. Cooper, eds., *Industrial Innovation in the Soviet Union* (New Haven and London: Yale University Press, 1982), p. 7.
3. Christopher Freeman, "The Role of Technical Change in National Economic Development," in A. Amin and J.B. Goddard, eds., *Technological Change, Industrial Restructuring and Regional Development* (London: Allen & Unwin, 1986), pp. 100–114.
4. Peter Hall and Ann Markusen, eds., *Silicon Landscapes* (Boston: Allen & Unwin, 1985), p. 147.
5. Louis Wells, "Economic Man and Engineering Man: Choice in a Low-Wage Country," *Public Policy* (Summer 1973): 319–342.
6. Sometime in 1987, Li Tieying apparently stepped down as the Minister of the Electronics Industry in terms of day-to-day responsibilities and seemingly spent most of his time in his capacity as Director of the State Commission for Restructuring of the Economy under the State Council. In April 1988, Li was officially appointed Minister of the State Education Commission. Premier Li Peng took over as the Director of the State Commission for Restructuring of the Economy. Zou Jiahua became the Minister of the Machine-Building and Electronics Industry.

APPENDIXES

APPENDIX

APPENDIX A

INSTITUTIONS VISITED IN SHANGHAI, JULY 1985

Shanghai Instruments Research Institute
Shanghai Components Factory #5
Shanghai Radio Factory #18
Shanghai Instruments and Electronics Import & Export Corporation
Shanghai Radio Factory #2
Shanghai Vacuum Tube Research Institute
Meeting with Shanghai S&T, Economic and Planning Commission,
    Office of Microelectronics and Computers, Society for Shanghai's
    Development Strategy, Shanghai Economic Zone Administration,
    Shanghai Economic Research Center
Instrumentation and Electronics Bureau
Shanghai Radio Factory #14
Shanghai Computer Factory
Shanghai Institute of Computing Technology
Shanghai Radio Factory #19
Great Wall Industrial Corporation
Shanghai Radio Equipment Factory
Shanghai Radio Factory #1
Chinese Academy of Social Sciences, Shanghai Branch, Economic, Legal
    and Consultancy Center
Shanghai Microcomputer Factory
Fudan University

Chinese Academy of Sciences, Institute of Metallurgy
Chinese Academy of Sciences, Institute of Ceramics
Shanghai Jiaotong University
Ministry of Electronics, East China Computer Research Institute
Shanghai Radio Factory #7
Shanghai Science and Technology Commission

AN OUTLINE OF THE HIGH TECHNOLOGY DEVELOPMENT PROGRAM IN CHINA

When Archimedes was exclaiming Eureka, Eureka, little did he realise that somewhere in the land of the East, people were discovering gunpowder and preparing it as rocket fuel. For centuries, the Chinese were the world technological leader and contributed a large share to mankind's knowledge. Yet, China must not rest on its laurels. Today, high technologies are developing in ways beyond the imagination of any but the rarest minds. High technologies are changing the patterns of production, fashioning industrial structure and generating a leapfrog in the social productive forces. A profound change is also under way in the styles of living. Developed countries, all of them, have committed great amount of resources in terms of manpower, materials and capital, regarding it as a national strategy for development.

Being a developing country, China cannot yet afford to undertake the full-scale development of high technologies in the immediate future. Yet, it is of paramount importance for it to take full advantage of modern science and technology in the service of the society and in attaining the strategic goal of quadrupling its national industrial and agricultural output by year 2000. To this end, we must mobilize most of our scientific and technological resources. Meanwhile, as high technologies will exert an enormous impact on the future economic growth and lay the ground

Source: The State Science and Technology Commission, Beijing, 1988.

for China's economic leap around the turn of the next century, they deserve our uttermost attention now.

As an immediate part of the strategic objectives within this century, China's high technology research and development constitute a component of the Seventh Five Year Plan (1986–1990). This introduction outlines the part that is planned to serve economic development at the close of this and start of the next centuries. The projects outlined herein aim to pool together the best technological resources in China over the next 15 years to keep up with international high technology development, bridge the gap between China and other countries in several most important areas, and wherever possible strive for breakthroughs. The program also aims to provide technological backup for economic development and train large numbers of talents for the future.

Seven priority research areas are included in this program—biotechnology, space technology, information technology, laser technology, automation technology, energy technology and advanced materials. Since China is at present not in a position to finance a comprehensive program, not even all branches within the seven areas, arrangements have been made on the basis of the country's actual capabilities and to give prominence to priorities.

In the seven areas mentioned above, more than a dozen major subjects have been selected, which will provide an umbrella for the development of other related disciplines and research branches. As for those projects that still require further studies to determine technical approaches, implementation will not start until a feasibility study proves they are in the right direction. In most cases, these projects will result in specific end-products. Only the very large ones will terminate with laboratory prototypes to be developed into industrial equipment or new products at a later stage according to the actual needs.

I.   Biotechnology

The objective is to improve people's health through better nutrition by early next century. The following areas are included:

1.   High-yield, High Quality and Adversity-Proof Animals and Plants

Directed breeding of new animal and plant varieties will be developed to increase the output of grain, meat, fish and milk. It is expected to obtain by the end of this century hybrids of sub-species of rice capable of averaging over one ton per mu in double cropping systems, new strains of high protein wheat, disease-insect resistant, high protein vegetable varieties, and high protein, draught-salinity tolerant herbage strains. Improvement will be made to enhance the symbiotic and associated nitrogen-fixation capacity of maize, soybean and vegatables so as to reduce the necessary amount of chemical fertilizers. New breeds of fast growing lean meat hogs, disease-resistant livestocks and poultry as well as disease-cold resistant fishes will be raised. Techniques for enhancing reproductivity of milk cows are also to be developed.

2. New Medicines, Vaccines and Genic Therapy

R&D will be conducted on new medicines and vaccines to prevent and cure malignant diseases of high incidence and danger which is beyond effective control in the near future. New medicines and bioproducts will be developed to control certain cancers, cardiovascular disease and major infectious diseases prevailing among people and animals. Bioprocessing engineering, product separation and purification techniques will be developed and utilized in production.

Research is to be carried out on genic diagnosis and therapy of some genetic diseases and tumors.

3. Protein Engineering

An advanced type of protein engineering through genetic engineering will be developed to provide new possibilities in the medical, chemical and food industries and agriculture.

II. Space Technology

Advanced launch vehicles with enhanced capacity will be developed to meet the growing demands for commercial launch services.

R&D will continue on space science and technology for peaceful purposes.

III. Information Technology

Emphasis will be focused on technologies promising significant breakthroughs and extensive application at the beginning of the next century.

1. Intelligent Computer Systems

Efforts will be made to develop computers with intelligent hierarchical structure and knowledge/intelligence processing capability, and to introduce man-machine interfaces in natural languages and software automation technology. The application of artificial intelligence will be promoted to lay the foundation for the intelligent computer industry.

2.   Optoelectronic Devices and Microelectronic/Optoelectronic Systems Integration Technology

Optoelectronic devices and systems integration technology will be developed for application in sensing, computation and telecommunication.

New approaches are to be studied for LSI fabrication in preparation, technologically and physically, for developing new types of information acquisition and processing systems, computers and telecommunication equipment.

3.   Information Acquisition and Processing Technology

To meet the needs of the new intelligent industrial automation systems, various information acquisition and processing technologies will be developed, with emphasis on new ways of acquisition and real-time image processing techniques. The application of information technology in various fields, such as resource exploration, weather forecast, marine monitoring, quality control in agriculture, forestry and industrial products.

IV.   Laser Technology

R&D will be carried out in laser technologies to achieve better quality and performance. Laboratory achievements shall be applied to material processing, plasma technology, pulse power technology, high resolution spectroscopy, etc.

V.   Automation Technology

1.   Computer Integrated Manufacturing System

In view of the needs for a new generation of automated production technology characterized by diversity of products, small batch production, high efficiency and quality, and quick response to market change and short product cycle, it is important to keep track of and undertake research on key technologies associated with the development of computer integrated manufacturing systems (CIMS) and build a demonstration production line.

2.   Intelligent Robots

Three types of intelligent robots will be developed for precision assembly, underwater operation and operation in adverse environments.

VI.   Energy Technology

1.   Coal-Fired MHD Power Generation Technology

Coal-fired MHD power generation technology will be developed to improve thermal conversion efficiency, conserve coal resources, fully utilize medium-grade and high-sulfur coals which are abundant in China, and to reduce the pollution and transportation associated with tradi-tional power generation through coal combustion.

2. Advanced Nuclear Reactor Technology

In view of the development of nuclear energy in the 21st century, a choice will be made to develop a safe, economically viable and highly fuel efficient type of reactor among fast breeder reactor, high tempera-ture gas cool reactor and fusion-fission hybrid reactor that uses existing fusion technology.

VII. Advanced Materials

The aim of developing advanced materials is to meet the requirement of research in this program.

The major items included are: (1) photo-electronic materials; (2) high-performance structural materials with corrosion resistance and light weight; (3) special functional materials; (4) high temperature-wear resistance and high strength composite materials; (5) research on special testing and measuring techniques.

Studies will be carried out, using microscopic structure theories at different levels, in modern materials science and technology combin-ing material design, research and application.

Policies and Implementation Measures

1. Coordination and Mobilizing Resources

In order to reach the projected objectives, the major subjects listed in the program will be studied and developed by the best available S&T forces, regardless of their departmental or regional affiliations. In addi-tion, the bidding system or selective commissioning will be introduced to ensure the tasks be given only to the best qualified units or individ-uals. Funds will be allocated along with projects, rather than distributed on an equalitarian basis to all departments or units.

The Science and Technology Leading Group of the State Council is responsible for making decisions and coordination on major issues.

2. Cooperation and Interlinkage

The program shall be implemented by fully utilizing the existing laboratories and equipment. Close lateral cooperation must be strength-ened. An effective form of such cooperation will be the establishment of flexible research institutions or joint development centers joined by project executing units so as to bring out the strength and potential of each organization.

The implementation of this program should be closely linked with programs and projects in other scientific and technological plans to complement each other and avoid unnecessary duplication. Research results in different phases and areas under different projects must be promptly transferred to other extension and application plans, to be turned into productive forces and yield economic benefits.

3.   The Important Role of Young and Middle-aged Experts

Since the present program extends to the end of this century, special attention should be given to the training of a younger generation of scientists and engineers. Efforts are to be made to find and give responsibilities to the outstanding ones so as to ensure the timely succession of the new to the old generation of scientists and engineers. It is necessary to select highly qualified young and middle-aged experts on a nationwide basis and put them on important posts. Those unqualified for their positions must be relieved of their duties timely, thus maintaining an active and efficient task force.

4.   Instituting a System of Well-defined Technical and Economic Responsibility

Project directors will be appointed for the technical and economic affairs of each project, giving them full authority and responsibilities in recruitment, planning, research assignment and fund allocation.

Expert committees and expert teams will be set up for research areas and major subjects respectively. The role of experts in consultation, assessment, decision making and policy guidance must be accorded full importance.

5.   International Cooperation

International cooperation shall be promoted in the implementation of this program on the basis of equality and mutual benefits, either through bilateral or multilateral channels, at governmental or non-governmental levels, and in various forms.

APPENDIX C

INVESTMENT PROCEDURES IN SHANGHAI'S CAOHEJING MICROELECTRONIC INDUSTRIAL PARK

Figure C-1.   Channels and Procedures of Examination and Approval to the Establishment of Joint Ventures Using Chinese and Foreign Investment.

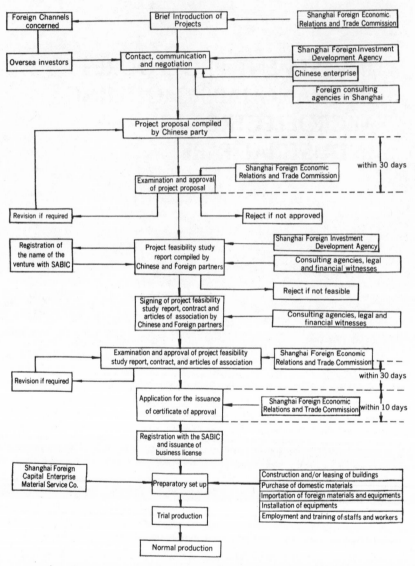

SABIC=Shanghai Administrative Bureau for Industry and Commerce

Source: "Investment Guide of Shanghai Caohejing Microelectronic Industrial Park," Shanghai Caohejing Microelectronic Industrial Park Development Corporation, Shanghai, 1988.

Figure C–2.   Channels and Procedures of Examination and Approval to the Establishment of Wholly Foreign-Owned Enterprises.

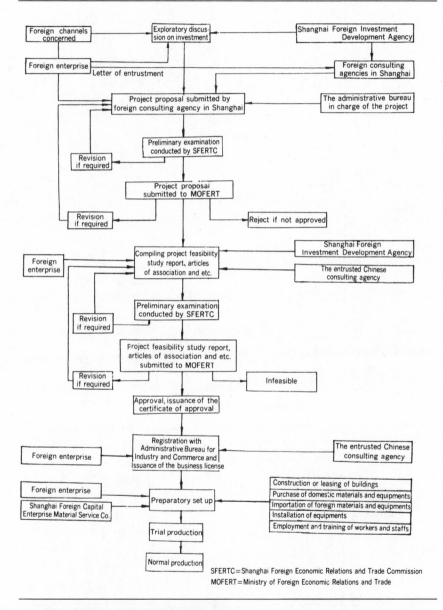

SFERTC=Shanghai Foreign Economic Relations and Trade Commission
MOFERT=Ministry of Foreign Economic Relations and Trade

Source: "Investment Guide of Shanghai Caohejing Microelectronic Industrial Park," Shanghai Caohejing Microelectronic Industrial Park Development Corporation, Shanghai, 1988.

Table C-1. List of Investment Procedures for Chinese-Foreign Joint Venture, Cooperation Project, or Enterprise Exclusively with Foreign Capital.

Investment Formalities	Documents Preparation	Referential Documents
1. Brief introduction of project Brief introduction of the intent of foreign investor	Brief introduction of the foreign investment project by the Chinese party Outline of the foreign investment project plan made by foreign investors Brief introduction of the foreign corporation	1. Shanghai • Investment Environment • Laws and Regulations 2. Trades hoping to absorb foreign capital in SMIP
2. Contact and discussion For investment exclusively with foreign capital, the investor of the project shall entrust Chinese agencies or consultant organizations to be agent and draw up project proposal	Status presentation by the two parties of the joint venture Written entrustment of projects exclusively with foreign capital Draw up project proposal	3. Main contents of the project proposal 4. The Law of the People's Republic of China on Joint Ventures Using Chinese and Foreign Investment 5. Regulations for the Implementation of the Law on Joint Ventures Using Chinese and Foreign Investment

3. Submit project proposal by Chinese party or the agencies	Project proposal Legal document of starting business made out by foreign trader's government or department concerned	6. Shanghai Overseas Investment Utilization Manual 7. Law on Enterprises Operated Exclusively with Foreign Capital
4. Apply for registration of enterprise's name to the Shanghai Administrative Bureau for Industry and Commerce	Written approval of project proposal	8. Provisions of Shanghai Municipality on Application and Approval of Chinese-Foreign Equity Joint Ventures, Chinese-Foreign Cooperative Ventures, and Enterprises Operated Exclusively with Foreign Capital
5. Chinese and foreign parties draw up and submit feasibility study report Project exclusively with foreign capital shall entrust an agent to draw up and submit feasibility study report	Finance, site and infrastructures construction should be included in feasibility study report Environment protection document The comment and letter of response from the department in charge	9. Main contents of the feasibility study report
6. Draw up enterprise charter, sign contract and submit them to the authorities concerned	Charter, contract, letter of attorney from the signer, list of the names of the board of directors	See 10, 11, 12

Table C–1. (continued)

Investment Formalities	Documents Preparation	Referential Documents
7. Apply for instrument of ratification	Submit application Investor's certificate Project proposal and instrument of ratification Feasibility study report and instrument of ratification Charter of enterprise List of the names of the board of directors Legal document of starting business made out by foreign trader's government	10. Measure of Shanghai Municipality on Labor Management in Joint Ventures Using Chinese and Foreign Investment (for Trial Implementation) 11. Regulations of Shanghai Municipality on Supply and Marketing of Materials and Price Control Concerning Joint Ventures Using Chinese and Foreign Investment (for Trial Implementation) 12. Procedures of Shanghai Municipality for Endowment Insurance for Chinese Employees in Chinese-Foreign Joint Ventures (for Trial Implementation) 13. Procedures of Shanghai Municipality for the Administration of the Use of Land in Chinese-Foreign Joint Ventures
8. Register with the Shanghai Administrative Bureau for Industry and Commerce and get business license	Application for registration Instrument of ratification issued by the Ministry of Foreign Economic Relations and Trade or Shanghai Municipal Government	

Feasibility study report, contract charter and documents of approval from authorities concerned

List of the names of the board of directors

Legal document of starting business made out by foreign trader's government

14. Regulations of Shanghai Municipality on Management of Construction Projects Contracted to Foreign Designing and Building Enterprises

9. Preparatory set up

Initial design and instrument of ratification

Construction license

Documents for supply of public utilities

List of import raw materials and equipment

Report on the recruiting staff and workers to the Shanghai Labor Bureau for record

Source: "Investment Guide of Shanghai Caohejing Microelectronic Industrial Park," Shanghai Caohejing Microelectronic Industrial Park Development Corporation, Shanghai, 1988.

SELECTED BIBLIOGRAPHY

BOOKS

Amin, A., and J.B. Goddard, eds. *Technological Change, Industrial Restructuring and Regional Development.* London: Allen & Unwin, 1986.

Amann, Ronald, and Julian Cooper. *Technical Progress and Soviet Economic Development.* Oxford: Blackwell, 1986.

Berliner, Joseph. *The Innovation Decision in the Soviet Industry.* Cambridge, Mass.: MIT Press, 1976.

Castells, Manuel, ed. *High Technology, Space and Society.* Beverly Hills: Sage Publications, 1985.

Forester, Thomas. *The Microelectronics Revolution.* Cambridge, Mass.: MIT Press, 1980.

———, ed. *The Information Technology Revolution,* Cambridge, Mass.: MIT Press, 1985.

Gregory, Gene. *Japanese Electronics Technology: Enterprise and Innovation.* Tokyo: Japan Times Press, 1985.

Hall, Peter, and Ann Markusen, eds. *Silicon Landscapes.* Boston: Allen & Unwin, 1985.

Hunt, V. Daniel. *Mechatronics: Japan's Newest Threat.* New York: Chapman and Hall, 1988.

Li Boxi et al. *Zhongguo Jishu Gaizao Wenti Yanjiu* (Analysis of the Problems Regarding China's Technical Transformation), 2 vols. Shanxi: People's Publishing House, 1984.

Malerba, Franco. *The Semiconductor Business.* Madison: The University of Wisconsin Press, 1985.

Ministry of Electronics Industry. *China Electronics Yearbook 1987.* Beijing: Ministry of Electronics Publishing House, 1987.

Nelson, Richard. *High Technology Policies: A Five Nation Comparison.* Washington, D.C.: American Enterprise Institute, 1984.

Orleans, Leo, ed. *Science in Contemporary China.* Stanford, Calif.: Stanford University Press, 1981.

Shanghai Jingji Fazhan Zhanlüe Wenji (Selections on Shanghai's Economic Development Strategy). Shanghai: Shanghai Academy of Social Sciences, 1984.

Shanghai Statistical Bureau. *Statistical Yearbook of Shanghai, 1987.* Shanghai: Shanghai People's Publishing House, 1987.

State Statistical Bureau. *Statistical Yearbook of China, 1986.* Beijing: State Statistical Bureau, 1987.

Suttmeier, Richard P. *Science, Technology and China's Drive for Modernization.* Stanford, Calif.: Hoover Institution Press, 1980.

U.S. Congress, Joint Economic Committee, *Chinese Economy Post-Mao,* 2 vols. Washington, D.C.: U.S. Government Printing Office, 1978.

———. *China Under the Four Modernizations,* 2 vols. Washington, D.C.: U.S. Government Printing Office, 1982.

———. *China's Economy Looks Toward the Year 2000,* 2 vols. Washington, D.C.: U.S. Government Printing Office, 1986.

Zhongguo Kexue Jishu Zhinan (Primer on China's S&T Policy). Beijing: S&T Publishing House, 1986.

ARTICLES

Dorfman, Nancy. "Route 128: The Development of a Regional High Technology Economy." *Research Policy,* December 1983, pp. 299–316.

"Electronics Industry Booming." *China Daily,* March 8, 1986, p. 4.

Feng Zhijun. "Research on Shanghai's Strategic Countermeasures for the New Technological Revolution." *Shijie Jingji Wenhui,* no. 4, 1984, pp. 32–38, translated in *Joint Publications Research Service—China Economic Affairs* 85–031, March 25, 1985, pp. 72–84.

"The Glorious Development of Shanghai's Electronics Industry from Scratch." *Wenhui Bao,* September 19, 1979.

Howe, Sam. "China's High Tech Troubles." *New York Times,* May 5, 1985, p. F9.

Li Peng. "The Electronics and Information Industries Should Serve the Construction of the Four Modernizations." *Jingji Ribao,* January 14, 1985.

Li Tieying. "Continue the Reform, Speed Up the Development, Actively Invigorate the Electronics Industry." *Zhongguo Dianzi Bao,* no. 59. January 21, 1986.

Lü Dong. "Report at the National Work Conference for Computer Applications." *Zhongguo Keji Bao,* no. 75, June 25, 1986.

Mowery, D., and N. Rosenberg. "The Influence of Market Demand upon Innovation: A Critical Review." *Research Policy,* April 1979, pp. 103–153.

"Push Vigorously the Domestic Production of Microcomputers During the Seventh Five-Year Plan." *Renmin Ribao,* July 21, 1986.

Simon, Denis Fred. "Rethinking R&D." *China Business Review,* July-August 1983, pp. 25–31.

—— and Detlef Rehn. "Understanding the Electronics Industry." *China Business Review,* March-April 1986, pp. 10–15.

Wang Yangyuan. "Discussion About the Technical Goals of China's IC Industry in the 1990s." *China Computerworld,* no. 9, May 8, 1984, p. 3.

"Why Is Shanghai's Development of New Products So Sluggish." *Shijie Jingji Daobao,* February 28, 1983, p. 10.

Xiu Jinya. "Push Vigorously the Research, Production and Application of Computers." *Jingji Guanli,* no. 2, 1984, pp. 12–15.

PERIODICALS

Beijing Review
China Business Review
China Computerworld
China Daily
Dianzi Shichang (Electronics Market)
Guangming Ribao (Guangming Daily)
Intertrade
Jingji Guanli (Economic Management)
Jixie Zhoubao (Machine-Building Weekly)
Kexuexue Yu Kexue Jishu Guanli (Science of Science and S&T Management)
Keyan Guanli (Research Management)
Research Policy
Renmin Ribao (People's Daily)
Wenhui Bao (Wenhui Daily)
Zhongguo Dianzi Bao (China Electronics Daily)
Zhongguo Keji Bao (China S&T Daily)

INDEX

ABOUT THE AUTHORS

Denis Fred Simon is an associate professor of international business and technology at the Fletcher School of Law and Diplomacy at Tufts University. Previously, he was the Ford International Assistant Professor of International Management at the Sloan School of Management at MIT. He has also served as a consultant to several major corporations engaged in business in China as well as with the Office of Technology Assessment, the Joint Economic Committee, the National Academy of Sciences, and the National Science Foundation. Professor Simon specializes in the study of international technology transfer and comparative business-government relations, with an emphasis on East Asia. He has been a frequent visitor to China and other parts of East Asia. He recently completed a study on technology transfer and foreign investment in Taiwan (*Taiwan, Technology Transfer and Transnationalism*) and a book manuscript (with Christopher Engholm) entitled *The China Venture: Corporate America Encounters the People's Republic of China*. He is also the author of numerous articles on science and technology in China and East Asia, China's computer industry, high-technology development in Taiwan and Korea, and technology transfer to China.

Detlef Rehn is a senior research associate at the Ostasien Institute in Bonn, West Germany. He has lived and studied in China. In recent years he has focused his attention on the problems of electronics development in China. He is the author of a monograph entitled *China Enters the Electronics Age: The Case of Changzhou.*